Tefal 2-Basket Air | cookbook 2024

Delicious, Affordable and Time-Saving Tefal Dual Zone Air Fryer Recipes for Home cooking using DualZone Technology

Daniela M. Lira

Warning-Disclaimer:

The purpose of this book is to educate and entertain. The author or publisher does not guarantee

that anyone following the techniques, suggestions, tips, ideas, or strategies will become successful.

The author and publisher shall have neither liability or responsibility to anyone with respect to any

loss or damage caused, or alleged to be caused, directly or indirectly by the information contained in

this book.

CONTENTS

MEASUREMENT CONVERSIONS

BASIC KITCHEN CONVERSIONS & EQUIVALENTS

DRY MEASUREMENTS CONVERSION

CHART

3 TEASPOONS = 1 TABLESPOON = 1/16 CUP

6 TEASPOONS = 2 TABLESPOONS = 1/8 CUP

12 TEASPOONS = 4 TABLESPOONS = 1/4 CUP

24 TEASPOONS = 8 TABLESPOONS = 1/2 CUP

36 TEASPOONS = 12 TABLESPOONS = 3/4 CUP

48 TEASPOONS = 16 TABLESPOONS = 1 CUP

METRIC TO US COOKING CONVER-SIONS

OVEN TEMPERATURES

120 °C = 250 °F

160 °C = 320 °F

180 °C = 350 °F

205 °C = 400 °F

220 °C = 425 °F

LIQUID MEASUREMENTS CONVERSION

CHART

8 FLUID OUNCES = 1 CUP = 1/2 PINT = 1/4 QUART

16 FLUID OUNCES = 2 CUPS = 1 PINT = 1/2 QUART

32 FLUID OUNCES = 4 CUPS = 2 PINTS = 1 QUART

1/4 GALLON

128 FLUID OUNCES = 16 CUPS = 8 PINTS = 4 QUARTS = 1 GALLON

BAKING IN GRAMS

1 CUP FLOUR = 140 GRAMS

1 CUP SUGAR = 150 GRAMS

1 CUP POWDERED SUGAR=160 GRAMS

1 CUP HEAVY CREAM = 235 GRAMS

VOLUME

1 MILLILITER=1/5 TEASPOON

5 ML = 1 TEASPOON

15 ML = 1 TABLESPOON

240 ML = 1 CUP OR 8 FLUID OUNCES

1 LITER=34 FL. OUNCES

WEIGHT

1 GRAM = 035 OUNCES

100 GRAMS=3.5 OUNCES

500 GRAMS = 1.1 POUNDS

1 KILOGRAM=35 OUNCES

US TO METRIC COOKING CONVERSIONS

1/5 TSP = 1 ML
1 TSP=5 ML
1 TBSP = 15 ML
1 FL OUNCE = 30 ML
1 CUP=237 ML
1 PINT (2 CUPS) = 473 ML
1 QUART (4 CUPS)=.95 LITER
1GALLON (16 CUPS)=3.8LITERS
1 0Z=28 GRAMS
1 POUND = 454 GRAMS

BUTTER

1 CUP BUTTER=2 STICKS = 8 OUNCES = 230 GRAMS=8 TABLESPOONS

WHAT DOES 1 CUP EQUAL

1 CUP = 8 FLUID OUNCES
1 CUP = 16 TABLESPOONS
1 CUP = 48 TEASPOONS
1 CUP = 1/2 PINT
1 CUP = 1/4 QUART
1 CUP = 1/16 GALLON
1 CUP = 240 ML

BAKING PAN CONVERSIONS

1 CUP ALL-PURPOSE FLOUR=4.5 OZ
1 CUP ROLLED OATS = 3 OZ 1 LARGE EGG = 1.7 OZ
1 CUP BUTTER=80Z 1 CUP MILK = 8 OZ
1 CUP HEAVY CREAM = 8.4 OZ
1 CUP GRANULATED SUGAR=7.1 OZ
1 CUP PACKED BROWN SUGAR = 7.75 OZ
1 CUP VEGETABLE OIL = 7.7 OZ
1 CUP UNSIFTED POWDERED SUGAR = 4.4 OZ

BAKING PAN CONVERSIONS

9-INCH ROUND CAKE PAN= 12 CUPS
10-INCH TUBE PAN =16 CUPS
11-INCH BUNDT PAN = 12 CUPS
9-INCH SPRINGFORM PAN = 10 CUPS
9 X 5 INCH LOAF PAN=8 CUPS
9-INCH SQUARE PAN=8 CUPS

Cajun Breakfast Sausage

Servings: 8
Cooking Time: 15 To 20 Minutes
Ingredients:

- 680 g 85% lean turkey mince
- 3 cloves garlic, finely chopped
- ¼ onion, grated
- 1 teaspoon Tabasco sauce
- 1 teaspoon Cajun seasoning
- 1 teaspoon dried thyme
- ½ teaspoon paprika
- ½ teaspoon cayenne

Directions:

1. Preheat the air fryer to 188ºC.
2. In a large bowl, combine the turkey, garlic, onion, Tabasco, Cajun seasoning, thyme, paprika, and cayenne. Mix with clean hands until thoroughly combined. Shape into 16 patties, about ½ inch thick.
3. Arrange the patties in a single layer in the two air fryer drawers. Pausing halfway through the cooking time to flip the patties, air fry for 15 to 20 minutes until a thermometer inserted into the thickest portion registers 74ºC.

Savory Soufflé

Servings: 4
Cooking Time: 8 Minutes
Ingredients:

- 4 tablespoons light cream
- 4 eggs
- 2 tablespoons fresh parsley, chopped
- 2 fresh red chilies pepper, chopped
- Salt, as required

Directions:

1. In a bowl, add all the ingredients and beat until well combined.
2. Divide the mixture into 4 greased soufflé dishes.
3. Press either "Zone 1" and "Zone 2" of Tefal 2-Basket Air Fryer and then rotate the knob to select "Air Fry".
4. Set the temperature to 200 degrees C, and then set the time for 5 minutes to preheat.
5. After preheating, arrange soufflé dishes into the basket.
6. Slide basket into Air Fryer and set the time for 8 minutes.

7. After cooking time is completed, remove the soufflé dishes from Air Fryer and serve warm.

Mozzarella Bacon Calzones

Servings: 4
Cooking Time: 12 Minutes
Ingredients:

- 2 large eggs
- 235 ml blanched finely ground almond flour
- 475 ml shredded Mozzarella cheese
- 60 g cream cheese, softened and broken into small pieces
- 4 slices cooked bacon, crumbled

Directions:

1. Beat eggs in a small bowl. Pour into a medium nonstick skillet over medium heat and scramble. Set aside.
2. In a large microwave-safe bowl, mix flour and Mozzarella. Add cream cheese to the bowl.
3. Place bowl in microwave and cook 45 seconds on high to melt cheese, then stir with a fork until a soft dough ball forms.
4. Cut a piece of parchment to fit air fryer drawer. Separate dough into two sections and press each out into an 8-inch round.
5. On half of each dough round, place half of the scrambled eggs and crumbled bacon. Fold the other side of the dough over and press to seal the edges.
6. Place calzones on ungreased parchment and into the zone 1 air fryer drawer. Adjust the temperature to 176ºC and set the timer for 12 minutes, turning calzones halfway through cooking. Crust will be golden and firm when done.
7. Let calzones cool on a cooking rack 5 minutes before serving.

Biscuit Balls

Servings: 6
Cooking Time: 18 Minutes.
Ingredients:
- 1 tablespoon butter
- 2 eggs, beaten
- ¼ teaspoon pepper
- 1 can (10.2-oz) Pillsbury Buttermilk biscuits
- 2 ounces cheddar cheese, diced into ten cubes
- Cooking spray
- Egg Wash
- 1 egg
- 1 tablespoon water

Directions:
1. Place a suitable non-stick skillet over medium-high heat and cook the bacon until crispy, then place it on a plate lined with a paper towel.
2. Melt butter in the same skillet over medium heat. Beat eggs with pepper in a bowl and pour them into the skillet.
3. Stir cook for 5 minutes, then remove it from the heat.
4. Add bacon and mix well.
5. Divide the dough into 5 biscuits and slice each into 2 layers.
6. Press each biscuit into 4-inch round.
7. Add a tablespoon of the egg mixture at the center of each round and top it with a piece of cheese.
8. Carefully fold the biscuit dough around the filling and pinch the edges to seal.
9. Whisk egg with water in a small bowl and brush the egg wash over the biscuits.
10. Place half of the biscuit bombs in each of the crisper plate and spray them with cooking oil.
11. Return the crisper plate to the Tefal Dual Zone Air Fryer.
12. Choose the Air Fry mode for Zone 1 and set the temperature to 375 degrees F and the time to 14 minutes.
13. Select the "MATCH" button to copy the settings for Zone 2.
14. Initiate cooking by pressing the START/STOP button.
15. Flip the egg bombs when cooked halfway through, then resume cooking.
16. Serve warm.

Nutrition:
- (Per serving) Calories 102 | Fat 7.6g |Sodium 545mg | Carbs 1.5g | Fiber 0.4g | Sugar 0.7g | Protein 7.1g

Double-dipped Mini Cinnamon Biscuits

Servings: 8 Biscuits
Cooking Time: 13 Minutes
Ingredients:
- 475 ml blanched almond flour
- 120 ml liquid or powdered sweetener
- 1 teaspoon baking powder
- ½ teaspoon fine sea salt
- 60 ml plus 2 tablespoons (¾ stick) very cold unsalted butter
- 60 ml unsweetened, unflavoured almond milk
- 1 large egg
- 1 teaspoon vanilla extract
- 3 teaspoons ground cinnamon
- Glaze:
- 120 ml powdered sweetener
- 60 ml double cream or unsweetened, unflavoured almond milk

Directions:
1. Preheat the air fryer to 175ºC. Line a pie pan that fits into your air fryer with parchment paper. 2. In a medium-sized bowl, mix together the almond flour, sweetener , baking powder, and salt. Cut the butter into ½-inch squares, then use a hand mixer to work the butter into the dry ingredients. When you are done, the mixture should still have chunks of butter. 3. In a small bowl, whisk together the almond milk, egg, and vanilla extract until blended. Using a fork, stir the wet ingredients into the dry ingredients until large clumps form. Add the cinnamon and use your hands to swirl it into the dough. 4. Form the dough into sixteen 1-inch balls and place them on the prepared pan, spacing them about ½ inch apart. Bake in the zone 1 air fryer basket until golden, 10 to 13 minutes. Remove from the air fryer and let cool on the pan for at least 5 minutes. 5. While the biscuits bake, make the glaze: Place the powdered sweetener in a small bowl and slowly stir in the heavy cream with a fork. 6. When the biscuits have cooled somewhat, dip the tops into the glaze, allow it to dry a bit, and then dip again for a thick glaze. 7. Serve warm or at room temperature. Store unglazed biscuits in an airtight container in the refrigerator for up to 3 days or in the freezer for up to a month. Reheat in a preheated 175ºC air fryer for 5 minutes, or until warmed through, and dip in the glaze as instructed above.

Banana Muffins

Servings: 10

Cooking Time: 15 Minutes

Ingredients:

- 2 very ripe bananas
- ⅓ cup olive oil
- 1 egg
- ½ cup brown sugar
- 1 teaspoon vanilla extract
- 1 teaspoon cinnamon
- ¾ cup self-rising flour

Directions:

1. In a large mixing bowl, mash the bananas, then add the egg, brown sugar, olive oil, and vanilla. To blend, stir everything together thoroughly.
2. Fold in the flour and cinnamon until everything is just blended.
3. Fill muffin molds evenly with the mixture (silicone or paper).
4. Install a crisper plate in both drawers. Place the muffin molds in a single layer in each drawer. Insert the drawers into the unit.
5. Select zone 1, select AIR FRY, set temperature to 360 degrees F/ 180 degrees C, and set time to 15 minutes. Select MATCH to match zone 2 settings to zone 1. Select START/STOP to begin.
6. Once the timer has finished, remove the muffins from the drawers.
7. Serve and enjoy!

Nutrition:

- (Per serving) Calories 148 | Fat 7.3g | Sodium 9mg | Carbs 19.8g | Fiber 1g | Sugar 10g | Protein 1.8g

Glazed Apple Fritters Glazed Peach Fritters

Servings:4

Cooking Time: 12 Minutes

Ingredients:

- FOR THE FRITTERS
- ¾ cup all-purpose flour
- 2 tablespoons granulated sugar
- 1 teaspoon baking powder
- ½ teaspoon kosher salt
- ½ teaspoon ground cinnamon
- ⅓ cup whole milk
- 2 tablespoons cold unsalted butter, grated
- 1 large egg
- 1 teaspoon fresh lemon juice
- 1 apple, peeled and diced
- 1 peach, peeled and diced
- FOR THE GLAZE
- ½ cup powdered sugar
- 1 tablespoon whole milk
- ½ teaspoon vanilla extract
- ½ teaspoon ground cinnamon
- Pinch salt

Directions:

1. To prep the fritters: In a large bowl, combine the flour, granulated sugar, baking powder, salt, and cinnamon. Stir in the milk, butter, egg, and lemon juice to form a thick batter.
2. Transfer half of the batter to a second bowl. Fold the apples into one bowl and the peaches into the other.
3. To prep the glaze: In a small bowl, whisk together the powdered sugar, milk, vanilla, cinnamon, and salt until smooth. Set aside.
4. To cook the fritters: Install a crisper plate in each of the two baskets. Drop two ¼-cup scoops of the apple fritter batter into the Zone 1 basket and insert the basket in the unit. Drop two ¼-cup scoops of the peach fritter batter into the Zone 2 basket and insert the basket in the unit.
5. Select Zone 1, select AIR FRY, set the temperature to 345°F, and set the time to 10 minutes.
6. Select Zone 2, select AIR FRY, set the temperature to 345°F, and set the time to 12 minutes. Select SMART FINISH.
7. Press START/PAUSE to begin cooking.
8. When cooking is complete, transfer the fritters to a wire rack and drizzle the glaze over them. Serve warm or at room temperature.

Nutrition:

- (Per serving) Calories: 298; Total fat: 8g; Saturated fat: 4.5g; Carbohydrates: 53g; Fiber: 3g; Protein: 5g; Sodium: 170mg

Bacon-and-eggs Avocado And Simple Scotch Eggs

Servings: 5
Cooking Time: 25 Minutes
Ingredients:
- Bacon-and-Eggs Avocado:
- 1 large egg
- 1 avocado, halved, peeled, and pitted
- 2 slices bacon
- Fresh parsley, for serving (optional)
- Sea salt flakes, for garnish (optional)
- Simple Scotch Eggs:
- 4 large hard boiled eggs
- 1 (340 g) package pork sausage meat
- 8 slices thick-cut bacon
- 4 wooden toothpicks, soaked in water for at least 30 minutes

Directions:
1. Make the Bacon-and-Eggs Avocado :
2. 1. Spray the zone 1 air fryer basket with avocado oil. Preheat the air fryer to 160°C. Fill a small bowl with cool water. Soft-boil the egg: Place the egg in the zone 1 air fryer basket. Air fry for 6 minutes for a soft yolk or 7 minutes for a cooked yolk. Transfer the egg to the bowl of cool water and let sit for 2 minutes. Peel and set aside. 3. Use a spoon to carve out extra space in the center of the avocado halves until the cavities are big enough to fit the soft-boiled egg. Place the soft-boiled egg in the center of one half of the avocado and replace the other half of the avocado on top, so the avocado appears whole on the outside. 4. Starting at one end of the avocado, wrap the bacon around the avocado to completely cover it. Use toothpicks to hold the bacon in place. 5. Place the bacon-wrapped avocado in the zone 1 air fryer basket and air fry for 5 minutes. Flip the avocado over and air fry for another 5 minutes, or until the bacon is cooked to your liking. Serve on a bed of fresh parsley, if desired, and sprinkle with salt flakes, if desired. 6. Best served fresh. Store extras in an airtight container in the fridge for up to 4 days. Reheat in a preheated 160°C air fryer for 4 minutes, or until heated through.
3. Make the Simple Scotch Eggs :
4. Slice the sausage meat into four parts and place each part into a large circle.
5. Put an egg into each circle and wrap it in the sausage. Put in the refrigerator for 1 hour.
6. Preheat the air fryer to 235°C.
7. Make a cross with two pieces of thick-cut bacon. Put a wrapped egg in the center, fold the bacon over top of the egg, and secure with a toothpick.
8. Air fry in the preheated zone 2 air fryer basket for 25 minutes.
9. Serve immediately.

Parmesan Ranch Risotto And Oat And Chia Porridge

Servings: 6
Cooking Time: 30 Minutes
Ingredients:
- Parmesan Ranch Risotto:
- 1 tablespoon olive oil
- 1 clove garlic, minced
- 1 tablespoon unsalted butter
- 1 onion, diced
- 180 ml Arborio rice
- 475 ml chicken stock, boiling
- 120 ml Parmesan cheese, grated
- Oat and Chia Porridge:
- 2 tablespoons peanut butter
- 4 tablespoons honey
- 1 tablespoon butter, melted
- 1 L milk
- 475 ml oats
- 235 ml chia seeds

Directions:
1. Make the Parmesan Ranch Risotto :
2. Preheat the air fryer to 200°C.
3. Grease a round baking tin with olive oil and stir in the garlic, butter, and onion.
4. Transfer the tin to the zone 1 air fryer basket and bake for 4 minutes. Add the rice and bake for 4 more minutes.
5. Turn the air fryer to 160°C and pour in the chicken stock. Cover and bake for 22 minutes.
6. Scatter with cheese and serve.
7. Make the Oat and Chia Porridge :
8. Preheat the air fryer to 200°C.
9. Put the peanut butter, honey, butter, and milk in a bowl and stir to mix. Add the oats and chia seeds and stir.
10. Transfer the mixture to a bowl and bake in the zone 2 air fryer basket for 5 minutes. Give another stir before serving.

Morning Egg Rolls

Servings: 6
Cooking Time: 13 Minutes.

Ingredients:

- 2 eggs
- 2 tablespoons milk
- Salt, to taste
- Black pepper, to taste
- ½ cup shredded cheddar cheese
- 2 sausage patties
- 6 egg roll wrappers
- 1 tablespoon olive oil
- 1 cup water

Directions:

1. Grease a small skillet with some olive oil and place it over medium heat.
2. Add sausage patties and cook them until brown.
3. Chop the cooked patties into small pieces. Beat eggs with salt, black pepper, and milk in a mixing bowl.
4. Grease the same skillet with 1 teaspoon of olive oil and pour the egg mixture into it.
5. Stir cook to make scrambled eggs.
6. Add sausage, mix well and remove the skillet from the heat.
7. Spread an egg roll wrapper on the working surface in a diamond shape position.
8. Add a tablespoon of cheese at the bottom third of the roll wrapper.
9. Top the cheese with egg mixture and wet the edges of the wrapper with water.
10. Fold the two corners of the wrapper and roll it, then seal the edges.
11. Repeat the same steps and divide the rolls in the two crisper plates.
12. Return the crisper plates to the Tefal Dual Zone Air Fryer.
13. Choose the Air Fry mode for Zone 1 and set the temperature to 375 degrees F and the time to 13 minutes.
14. Select the "MATCH" button to copy the settings for Zone 2.
15. Initiate cooking by pressing the START/STOP button.
16. Flip the rolls after 8 minutes and continue cooking for another 5 minutes.
17. Serve warm and fresh.

Nutrition:

- (Per serving) Calories 282 | Fat 15g |Sodium 526mg | Carbs 20g | Fiber 0.6g | Sugar 3.3g | Protein 16g

Onion Omelette And Buffalo Egg Cups

Servings: 4
Cooking Time: 15 Minutes

Ingredients:

- Onion Omelette:
- 3 eggs
- Salt and ground black pepper, to taste
- ½ teaspoons soy sauce
- 1 large onion, chopped
- 2 tablespoons grated Cheddar cheese
- Cooking spray
- Buffalo Egg Cups:
- 4 large eggs
- 60 g full-fat cream cheese
- 2 tablespoons buffalo sauce
- 120 ml shredded sharp Cheddar cheese

Directions:

1. Make the Onion Omelette :
2. Preheat the zone 1 air fryer drawer to 180ºC.
3. In a bowl, whisk together the eggs, salt, pepper, and soy sauce.
4. Spritz a small pan with cooking spray. Spread the chopped onion across the bottom of the pan, then transfer the pan to the zone 1 air fryer drawer.
5. Bake in the preheated air fryer for 6 minutes or until the onion is translucent.
6. Add the egg mixture on top of the onions to coat well. Add the cheese on top, then continue baking for another 6 minutes.
7. Allow to cool before serving.
8. Make the Buffalo Egg Cups :
9. Crack eggs into two ramekins.
10. In a small microwave-safe bowl, mix cream cheese, buffalo sauce, and Cheddar. Microwave for 20 seconds and then stir. Place a spoonful into each ramekin on top of the eggs.
11. Place ramekins into the zone 2 air fryer drawer.
12. Adjust the temperature to 160ºC and bake for 15 minutes.
13. Serve warm.

Simple Bagels

Servings: 4
Cooking Time: 12 Minutes
Ingredients:

- 125g plain flour
- 2 teaspoons baking powder
- Salt, as required
- 240g plain Greek yogurt
- 1 egg, beaten
- 1 tablespoon water
- 1 tablespoon sesame seeds
- 1 teaspoon coarse salt

Directions:

1. In a large bowl, mix together the flour, baking powder and salt.
2. Add the yogurt and mix until a dough ball forms.
3. Place the dough onto a lightly floured surface and then cut into 4 equal-sized balls.
4. Roll each ball into a 17 – 19 cm rope and then join ends to shape a bagel.
5. Grease basket of Tefal 2-Basket Air Fryer.
6. Press your chosen zone - "Zone 1" or "Zone 2" and then rotate the knob to select "Air Fry".
7. Set the temperature to 165 degrees C and then set the time for 5 minutes to preheat.
8. Meanwhile, in a small bowl, add egg and water and mix well.
9. Brush the bagels with egg mixture evenly.
10. Sprinkle the top of each bagel with sesame seeds and salt, pressing lightly.
11. After preheating, arrange 2 bagels into the basket of each zone.
12. Slide the basket into the Air Fryer and set the time for 12 minutes.
13. After cooking time is completed, remove the bagels from Air Fryer and serve warm.

Sausage Breakfast Casserole

Servings: 4
Cooking Time: 10 Minutes
Ingredients:

- 455g hash browns
- 455g ground breakfast sausage
- 1 green capsicum diced
- 1 red capsicum diced
- 1 yellow capsicum diced
- ¼ cup sweet onion diced
- 4 eggs

Directions:

1. Layer each air fryer basket with parchment paper.
2. Place the hash browns in both the baskets.
3. Spread sausage, onion and peppers over the hash brown.
4. Return the air fryer basket 1 to Zone 1, and basket 2 to Zone 2 of the Tefal 2-Basket Air Fryer.
5. Choose the "Air Fry" mode for Zone 1 at 355 degrees F temperature and 10 minutes of cooking time.
6. Select the "MATCH COOK" option to copy the settings for Zone 2.
7. Initiate cooking by pressing the START/PAUSE BUTTON.
8. Beat eggs in a bowl and pour over the air fried veggies.
9. Continue air frying for 10 minutes.
10. Garnish with salt and black pepper.
11. Serve warm.

Nutrition:

- (Per serving) Calories 267 | Fat 12g |Sodium 165mg | Carbs 39g | Fiber 1.4g | Sugar 22g | Protein 3.3g

Donuts

Servings: 6
Cooking Time: 15 Minutes
Ingredients:

- 1 cup granulated sugar
- 2 tablespoons ground cinnamon
- 1 can refrigerated flaky buttermilk biscuits
- ¼ cup unsalted butter, melted

Directions:

1. Combine the sugar and cinnamon in a small shallow bowl and set aside.
2. Remove the biscuits from the can and put them on a chopping board, separated. Cut holes in the center of each biscuit with a 1-inch round biscuit cutter (or a similarly sized bottle cap).
3. Place a crisper plate in each drawer. In each drawer, place 4 biscuits in a single layer. Insert the drawers into the unit.
4. Select zone 1, then AIR FRY, then set the temperature to 360 degrees F/ 180 degrees C with a 10-minute timer. To match zone 2 settings to zone 1, choose MATCH. To begin cooking, select START/STOP.
5. Remove the donuts from the drawers after the timer has finished.

Nutrition:

- (Per serving) Calories 223 | Fat 8g | Sodium 150mg | Carbs 40g | Fiber 1.4g | Sugar 34.2g | Protein 0.8g

Spinach And Red Pepper Egg Cups With Coffee-glazed Canadian Bacon

Servings:6
Cooking Time: 13 Minutes
Ingredients:
- FOR THE EGG CUPS
- 4 large eggs
- ¼ cup heavy (whipping) cream
- ¼ teaspoon kosher salt
- ¼ teaspoon freshly ground black pepper
- ½ cup roasted red peppers (about 1 whole pepper), drained and chopped
- ½ cup baby spinach, chopped
- FOR THE CANADIAN BACON
- ¼ cup brewed coffee
- 2 tablespoons maple syrup
- 1 tablespoon light brown sugar
- 6 slices Canadian bacon

Directions:
1. To prep the egg cups: In a medium bowl, whisk together the eggs and cream until well combined with a uniform, light color. Stir in the salt, black pepper, roasted red peppers, and spinach until combined.
2. Divide the egg mixture among 6 silicone muffin cups.
3. To prep the Canadian bacon: In a small bowl, whisk together the coffee, maple syrup, and brown sugar.
4. Using a basting brush, brush the glaze onto both sides of each slice of bacon.
5. To cook the egg cups and Canadian bacon: Install a crisper plate in each of the two baskets. Place the egg cups in the Zone 1 basket and insert the basket in the unit. Place the glazed bacon in the Zone 2 basket, making sure the slices don't overlap, and insert the basket in the unit. It is okay if the bacon overlaps a little bit.
6. Select Zone 1, select BAKE, set the temperature to 325°F, and set the time to 13 minutes.
7. Select Zone 2, select AIR FRY, set the temperature to 400°F, and set the time to 5 minutes. Select SMART FINISH.
8. Press START/PAUSE to begin cooking.
9. When the Zone 2 timer reads 2 minutes, press START/PAUSE. Remove the basket and use silicone-tipped tongs to flip the bacon. Reinsert the basket and press START/PAUSE to resume cooking.
10. When cooking is complete, serve the egg cups with the Canadian bacon.

Nutrition:
- (Per serving) Calories: 180; Total fat: 9.5g; Saturated fat: 4.5g; Carbohydrates: 9g; Fiber: 0g; Protein: 14g; Sodium: 688mg

Spinach And Swiss Frittata With Mushrooms

Servings: 4
Cooking Time: 20 Minutes
Ingredients:
- Olive oil cooking spray
- 8 large eggs
- ½ teaspoon salt
- ½ teaspoon black pepper
- 1 garlic clove, minced
- 475 ml fresh baby spinach
- 110 g baby mushrooms, sliced
- 1 shallot, diced
- 120 ml shredded Swiss cheese, divided
- Hot sauce, for serving (optional)

Directions:
1. Lightly coat the inside of a 6-inch round cake pan with olive oil cooking spray. In a large bowl, beat the eggs, salt, pepper, and garlic for 1 to 2 minutes, or until well combined.
2. Fold in the spinach, mushrooms, shallot, and 60 ml the Swiss cheese. Pour the egg mixture into the prepared cake pan, and sprinkle the remaining 60 ml Swiss over the top. Place into the zone 1 drawer.
3. Select Bake button and adjust temperature to 180°C, set time to 18 to 20 minutes and press Start. After the end, remove from the air fryer and allow to cool for 5 minutes. Drizzle with hot sauce before serving.

Broccoli-mushroom Frittata And Chimichanga Breakfast Burrito

Servings: 4
Cooking Time: 20 Minutes
Ingredients:

- Broccoli-Mushroom Frittata:
- 1 tablespoon olive oil
- 350 ml broccoli florets, finely chopped
- 120 ml sliced brown mushrooms
- 60 ml finely chopped onion
- ½ teaspoon salt
- ¼ teaspoon freshly ground black pepper
- 6 eggs
- 60 ml Parmesan cheese
- Chimichanga Breakfast Burrito:
- 2 large (10- to 12-inch) flour tortillas
- 120 ml canned refried beans (pinto or black work equally well)
- 4 large eggs, cooked scrambled
- 4 corn tortilla chips, crushed
- 120 ml grated chili cheese
- 12 pickled jalapeño slices
- 1 tablespoon vegetable oil
- Guacamole, salsa, and sour cream, for serving (optional)

Directions:

1. Make the Broccoli-Mushroom Frittata :
2. In a nonstick cake pan, combine the olive oil, broccoli, mushrooms, onion, salt, and pepper. Stir until the vegetables are thoroughly coated with oil. Place the cake pan in the zone 1 air fryer basket and set the air fryer to 205°C. Air fry for 5 minutes until the vegetables soften.
3. Meanwhile, in a medium bowl, whisk the eggs and Parmesan until thoroughly combined. Pour the egg mixture into the pan and shake gently to distribute the vegetables. Air fry for another 15 minutes until the eggs are set.
4. Remove from the air fryer and let sit for 5 minutes to cool slightly. Use a silicone spatula to gently lift the frittata onto a plate before serving.
5. Make the Chimichanga Breakfast Burrito :
6. Place the tortillas on a work surface and divide the refried beans between them, spreading them in a rough rectangle in the center of the tortillas. Top the beans with the scrambled eggs, crushed chips, cheese, and jalapeños. Fold one side over the fillings, then fold in each short side and roll up the rest of the way like a burrito.
7. Brush the outside of the burritos with the oil, then transfer to the zone 2 air fryer basket, seam-side down. Air fry at 175°C until the tortillas are browned and crisp and the filling is warm throughout, about 10 minutes.
8. Transfer the chimichangas to plates and serve warm with guacamole, salsa, and sour cream, if you like.

Sweet Potato Hash

Servings: 4
Cooking Time: 15 Minutes
Ingredients:

- 3 sweet potatoes, peel & cut into ½-inch pieces
- ½ tsp cinnamon
- 2 tbsp olive oil
- 1 bell pepper, cut into ½-inch pieces
- ½ tsp dried thyme
- ½ tsp nutmeg
- 1 medium onion, cut into ½-inch pieces
- Pepper
- Salt

Directions:

1. In a bowl, toss sweet potatoes with the remaining ingredients.
2. Insert a crisper plate in Tefal air fryer baskets.
3. Add potato mixture in both baskets.
4. Select zone 1 then select "air fry" mode and set the temperature to 355 degrees F for 15 minutes. Press "match" to match zone 2 settings to zone 1. Press "start/stop" to begin.

Nutrition:

- (Per serving) Calories 167 | Fat 7.3g |Sodium 94mg | Carbs 24.9g | Fiber 4.2g | Sugar 6.8g | Protein 2.2g

Baked Mushroom And Mozzarella Frittata With Breakfast Potatoes

Servings:4
Cooking Time: 35 Minutes
Ingredients:

- FOR THE FRITTATA
- 8 large eggs
- ⅓ cup whole milk
- 1 teaspoon kosher salt
- ½ teaspoon freshly ground black pepper
- 1 cup sliced cremini mushrooms (about 2 ounces)
- 1 teaspoon olive oil
- 2 ounces part-skim mozzarella cheese, cut into ½-inch cubes
- FOR THE POTATOES
- 2 russet potatoes, cut into ½-inch cubes
- 1 tablespoon olive oil
- ½ teaspoon garlic powder
- ¼ teaspoon kosher salt
- ¼ teaspoon freshly ground black pepper

Directions:

1. To prep the frittata: In a large bowl, whisk together the eggs, milk, salt, and pepper. Stir in the mushrooms.
2. To prep the potatoes: In a large bowl, combine the potatoes, olive oil, garlic powder, salt, and black pepper.
3. To cook the frittata and potatoes: Brush the bottom of the Zone 1 basket with 1 teaspoon of olive oil. Add the egg mixture to the basket, top with the mozzarella cubes, and insert the basket in the unit. Install a crisper plate in the Zone 2 basket. Place the potatoes in the basket and insert the basket in the unit.
4. Select Zone 1, select BAKE, set the temperature to 350°F, and set the time to 30 minutes.
5. Select Zone 2, select AIR FRY, set the temperature to 400°F, and set the time to 35 minutes. Select SMART FINISH.
6. Press START/PAUSE to begin cooking.
7. When the Zone 2 timer reads 15 minutes, press START/PAUSE. Remove the basket and shake the potatoes for 10 seconds. Reinsert the basket and press START/PAUSE to resume cooking.
8. When cooking is complete, the frittata will pull away from the edges of the basket and the potatoes will be golden brown. Transfer the frittata to a cutting board and cut into 4 portions. Serve with the potatoes.

Nutrition:

- (Per serving) Calories: 307; Total fat: 17g; Saturated fat: 5.5g; Carbohydrates: 18g; Fiber: 1g; Protein: 19g; Sodium: 600mg

Easy Sausage Pizza

Servings: 4
Cooking Time: 6 Minutes
Ingredients:

- 2 tablespoons ketchup
- 1 pitta bread
- 80 ml sausage meat
- 230 g Mozzarella cheese
- 1 teaspoon garlic powder
- 1 tablespoon olive oil

Directions:

1. Preheat the air fryer to 170°C.
2. Spread the ketchup over the pitta bread.
3. Top with the sausage meat and cheese. Sprinkle with the garlic powder and olive oil.
4. Put the pizza in the zone 1 air fryer basket and bake for 6 minutes.
5. Serve warm.

Beef, Pork, And Lamb Recipes

Rosemary Ribeye Steaks And Mongolian-style Beef

Servings: 6
Cooking Time: 15 Minutes
Ingredients:
- Rosemary Ribeye Steaks:
- 60 ml butter
- 1 clove garlic, minced
- Salt and ground black pepper, to taste
- 1½ tablespoons balsamic vinegar
- 60 ml rosemary, chopped
- 2 ribeye steaks
- Mongolian-Style Beef:
- Oil, for spraying
- 60 ml cornflour
- 450 g bavette or skirt steak, thinly sliced
- 180 ml packed light brown sugar
- 120 ml soy sauce
- 2 teaspoons toasted sesame oil
- 1 tablespoon minced garlic
- ½ teaspoon ground ginger
- 120 ml water
- Cooked white rice or ramen noodles, for serving

Directions:
1. Make the Rosemary Ribeye Steaks :
2. Melt the butter in a skillet over medium heat. Add the garlic and fry until fragrant.
3. Remove the skillet from the heat and add the salt, pepper, and vinegar. Allow it to cool.
4. Add the rosemary, then pour the mixture into a Ziploc bag.
5. Put the ribeye steaks in the bag and shake well, coating the meat well. Refrigerate for an hour, then allow to sit for a further twenty minutes.
6. Preheat the zone 1 air fryer drawer to 204°C.
7. Air fry the ribeye steaks for 15 minutes.
8. Take care when removing the steaks from the air fryer and plate up.
9. Serve immediately.
10. Make the Mongolian-Style Beef :
11. Line the zone 2 air fryer drawer with parchment and spray lightly with oil.
12. Place the cornflour in a bowl and dredge the steak until evenly coated. Shake off any excess cornflour.
13. Place the steak in the prepared drawer and spray lightly with oil.
14. Roast at 200°C for 5 minutes, flip, and cook for another 5 minutes.
15. In a small saucepan, combine the brown sugar, soy sauce, sesame oil, garlic, ginger, and water and bring to a boil over medium-high heat, stirring frequently. Remove from the heat.
16. Transfer the meat to the sauce and toss until evenly coated. Let sit for about 5 minutes so the steak absorbs the flavors. Serve with white rice or ramen noodles.

Rosemary And Garlic Lamb Chops

Servings: 4
Cooking Time: 15 Minutes
Ingredients:
- 8 lamb chops
- 3 tablespoons olive oil
- 2 tablespoons chopped fresh rosemary
- 1 teaspoon garlic powder or 3 cloves garlic, minced
- 1 teaspoon salt, or to taste
- ½ teaspoon black pepper, or to taste

Directions:
1. Dry the lamb chops with a paper towel.
2. Combine the olive oil, rosemary, garlic, salt, and pepper in a large mixing bowl. Toss the lamb in the marinade gently to coat it. Cover and set aside to marinate for 1 hour or up to overnight.
3. Install a crisper plate in both drawers. Place half the lamb chops in the zone 1 drawer and half in zone 2's, then insert the drawers into the unit.
4. Select zone 1, select AIR FRY, set temperature to 390 degrees F/ 200 degrees C, and set time to 15 minutes. Select MATCH to match zone 2 settings to zone 1. Press the START/STOP button to begin cooking.
5. When the time reaches 10 minutes, press START/STOP to pause the unit. Remove the drawers and flip the chops. Re-insert the drawers into the unit and press START/STOP to resume cooking.
6. Serve and enjoy!
Nutrition:
- (Per serving) Calories 427 | Fat 34g | Sodium 668mg | Carbs 1g | Fiber 1g | Sugar 1g | Protein 31g

Sausage And Cauliflower Arancini

Servings: 6
Cooking Time: 28 To 32 Minutes

Ingredients:

- Avocado oil spray
- 170 g Italian-seasoned sausage, casings removed
- 60 ml diced onion
- 1 teaspoon minced garlic
- 1 teaspoon dried thyme
- Sea salt and freshly ground black pepper, to taste
- 120 ml cauliflower rice
- 85 g cream cheese
- 110 g Cheddar cheese, shredded
- 1 large egg
- 120 ml finely ground blanched almond flour
- 60 ml finely grated Parmesan cheese
- Keto-friendly marinara sauce, for serving

Directions:

1. Spray a large skillet with oil and place it over medium-high heat. Once the skillet is hot, put the sausage in the skillet and cook for 7 minutes, breaking up the meat with the back of a spoon.

2. Reduce the heat to medium and add the onion. Cook for 5 minutes, then add the garlic, thyme, and salt and pepper to taste. Cook for 1 minute more.

3. Add the cauliflower rice and cream cheese to the skillet. Cook for 7 minutes, stirring frequently, until the cream cheese melts and the cauliflower is tender.

4. Remove the skillet from the heat and stir in the Cheddar cheese. Using a cookie scoop, form the mixture into 1½-inch balls. Place the balls on a parchment paper-lined baking sheet. Freeze for 30 minutes.

5. Place the egg in a shallow bowl and beat it with a fork. In a separate bowl, stir together the almond flour and Parmesan cheese.

6. Dip the cauliflower balls into the egg, then coat them with the almond flour mixture, gently pressing the mixture to the balls to adhere.

7. Set the air fryer to 204°C. Spray the cauliflower rice balls with oil, and arrange them in a single layer in the two air fryer drawers. Air fry for 5 minutes. Flip the rice balls and spray them with more oil. Air fry for 3 to 7 minutes longer, until the balls are golden brown.

8. Serve warm with marinara sauce.

Kielbasa Sausage With Pineapple And Kheema Meatloaf

Servings: 6 To 8
Cooking Time: 15 Minutes

Ingredients:

- Kielbasa Sausage with Pineapple:
- 340 g kielbasa sausage, cut into ½-inch slices
- 1 (230 g) can pineapple chunks in juice, drained
- 235 ml pepper chunks
- 1 tablespoon barbecue seasoning
- 1 tablespoon soy sauce
- Cooking spray
- Kheema Meatloaf:
- 450 g 85% lean beef mince
- 2 large eggs, lightly beaten
- 235 ml diced brown onion
- 60 ml chopped fresh coriander
- 1 tablespoon minced fresh ginger
- 1 tablespoon minced garlic
- 2 teaspoons garam masala
- 1 teaspoon coarse or flaky salt
- 1 teaspoon ground turmeric
- 1 teaspoon cayenne pepper
- ½ teaspoon ground cinnamon
- ⅛ teaspoon ground cardamom

Directions:

1. Make the Kielbasa Sausage with Pineapple :

2. Preheat the air fryer to 200°C. Spritz the zone 1 air fryer drawer with cooking spray.

3. Combine all the ingredients in a large bowl. Toss to mix well.

4. Pour the sausage mixture in the preheated zone 1 air fryer drawer.

5. Air fry for 10 minutes or until the sausage is lightly browned and the pepper and pineapple are soft. Shake the drawer halfway through. Serve immediately.

6. Make the Kheema Meatloaf :

7. In a large bowl, gently mix the beef mince, eggs, onion, coriander, ginger, garlic, garam masala, salt, turmeric, cayenne, cinnamon, and cardamom until thoroughly combined.

8. Place the seasoned meat in a baking pan. Place the pan in the zone 2 air fryer drawer. Set the temperature to 176°C for 15 minutes. Use a meat thermometer to ensure the meat loaf has reached an internal temperature of 72°C .

9. Drain the fat and liquid from the pan and let stand for 5 minutes before slicing.

10. Slice and serve hot.

Pork With Green Beans And Potatoes

Servings: 4
Cooking Time: 15 Minutes.
Ingredients:

- ¼ cup Dijon mustard
- 2 tablespoons brown sugar
- 1 teaspoon dried parsley flake
- ½ teaspoon dried thyme
- ¼ teaspoons salt
- ¼ teaspoons black pepper
- 1 ¼ lbs. pork tenderloin
- ¾ lb. small potatoes halved
- 1 (12-oz) package green beans, trimmed
- 1 tablespoon olive oil
- Salt and black pepper ground to taste

Directions:

1. Preheat your Air Fryer Machine to 400 degrees F.
2. Add mustard, parsley, brown sugar, salt, black pepper, and thyme in a large bowl, then mix well.
3. Add tenderloin to the spice mixture and coat well.
4. Toss potatoes with olive oil, salt, black pepper, and green beans in another bowl.
5. Place the prepared tenderloin in the crisper plate.
6. Return this crisper plate to the Zone 1 of the Tefal Dual Zone Air Fryer.
7. Choose the Air Fry mode for Zone 1 and set the temperature to 390 degrees F and the time to 15 minutes.
8. Add potatoes and green beans to the Zone 2.
9. Choose the Air Fry mode for Zone 2 with 350 degrees F and the time to 10 minutes.
10. Press the SYNC button to sync the finish time for both Zones.
11. Initiate cooking by pressing the START/STOP button.
12. Serve the tenderloin with Air Fried potatoes

Nutrition:

- (Per serving) Calories 400 | Fat 32g |Sodium 721mg | Carbs 2.6g | Fiber 0g | Sugar 0g | Protein 27.4g

Pork Tenderloin With Brown Sugar–pecan Sweet Potatoes

Servings:4
Cooking Time: 45 Minutes
Ingredients:

- FOR THE PORK TENDERLOIN
- 1½ pounds pork tenderloin
- 2 teaspoons vegetable oil
- ½ teaspoon kosher salt
- ½ teaspoon poultry seasoning
- FOR THE SWEET POTATOES
- 4 teaspoons unsalted butter, at room temperature
- 2 tablespoons dark brown sugar
- ¼ cup chopped pecans
- 4 small sweet potatoes

Directions:

1. To prep the pork: Coat the pork tenderloin with the oil, then rub with the salt and poultry seasoning.
2. To prep the sweet potatoes: In a small bowl, mix the butter, brown sugar, and pecans until well combined.
3. To cook the pork and sweet potatoes: Install a crisper plate in the Zone 1 basket. Place the pork tenderloin in the basket and insert the basket in the unit. Place the sweet potatoes in the Zone 2 basket and insert the basket in the unit.
4. Select Zone 1, select AIR FRY, set the temperature to 390°F, and set the time to 25 minutes.
5. Select Zone 2, select BAKE, set the temperature to 400°F, and set the time to 45 minutes. Select SMART FINISH.
6. Press START/PAUSE to begin cooking.
7. When the Zone 2 timer reads 10 minutes, press START/PAUSE. Remove the basket. Slice the sweet potatoes open lengthwise. Divide the pecan mixture among the potatoes. Reinsert the basket and press START/PAUSE to resume cooking.
8. When cooking is complete, the pork will be cooked through (an instant-read thermometer should read 145°F) and the potatoes will be soft and their flesh fluffy.
9. Transfer the pork loin to a plate or cutting board and let rest for at least 5 minutes before slicing and serving.

Nutrition:

- (Per serving) Calories: 415; Total fat: 15g; Saturated fat: 4.5g; Carbohydrates: 33g; Fiber: 4.5g; Protein: 36g; Sodium: 284mg

Honey Glazed Bbq Pork Ribs

Servings: 4
Cooking Time: 30 Minutes
Ingredients:

- 2 pounds pork ribs
- ¼ cup honey, divided
- 1 cup BBQ sauce
- ½ teaspoon garlic powder
- 2 tablespoons tomato ketchup
- 1 tablespoon Worcestershire sauce
- 1 tablespoon low-sodium soy sauce
- Freshly ground white pepper, as required

Directions:

1. In a bowl, mix together honey and the remaining ingredients except pork ribs.
2. Add the pork ribs and coat with the mixture generously.
3. Refrigerate to marinate for about 20 minutes.
4. Grease each basket of "Zone 1" and "Zone 2" of Tefal 2-Basket Air Fryer.
5. Press "Zone 1" and "Zone 2" and then rotate the knob for each zone to select "Air Fry".
6. Set the temperature to 355 degrees F/ 180 degrees C for both zones and then set the time for 5 minutes to preheat.
7. After preheating, arrange the ribs into the basket of each zone.
8. Slide each basket into Air Fryer and set the time for 26 minutes.
9. While cooking, flip the ribs once halfway through.
10. After cooking time is completed, remove the ribs from Air Fryer and place onto serving plates.
11. Drizzle with the remaining honey and serve immediately.

Simple Beef Sirloin Roast

Servings: 16
Cooking Time: 50 Minutes
Ingredients:

- 2 (2½-pound) sirloin roast
- Salt and ground black pepper, as required

Directions:

1. Grease each basket of "Zone 1" and "Zone 2" of Tefal 2-Basket Air Fryer.
2. Press "Zone 1" and "Zone 2" and then rotate the knob for each zone to select "Roast".
3. Set the temperature to 350 degrees F/ 175 degrees C for both zones and then set the time for 5 minutes to preheat.
4. Rub ach roast with salt and black pepper generously.
5. After preheating, arrange 1 roast into the basket of each zone.
6. Slide each basket into Air Fryer and set the time for 50 minutes.
7. After cooking time is completed, remove each roast from Air Fryer and place onto a platter for about 10 minutes before slicing.
8. With a sharp knife, cut each roast into desired-sized slices and serve.

Garlic Butter Steaks

Servings: 2
Cooking Time: 25 Minutes
Ingredients:

- 2 (6 ounces each) sirloin steaks or ribeyes
- 2 tablespoons unsalted butter
- 1 clove garlic, crushed
- ½ teaspoon dried parsley
- ½ teaspoon dried rosemary
- Salt and pepper, to taste

Directions:

1. Season the steaks with salt and pepper and set them to rest for about 2 hours before cooking.
2. Put the butter in a bowl. Add the garlic, parsley, and rosemary. Allow the butter to soften.
3. Whip together with a fork or spoon once the butter has softened.
4. When you're ready to cook, install a crisper plate in both drawers. Place the sirloin steaks in a single layer in each drawer. Insert the drawers into the unit.
5. Select zone 1, select AIR FRY, set temperature to 360 degrees F/ 180 degrees C, and set time to 10 minutes. Select MATCH to match zone 2 settings to zone 1. Select START/STOP to begin.
6. Once done, serve with the garlic butter.

Nutrition:

- (Per serving) Calories 519 | Fat 36g | Sodium 245mg | Carbs 1g | Fiber 0g | Sugar 0g | Protein 46g

Honey-baked Pork Loin

Servings: 6
Cooking Time: 22 To 25 Minutes
Ingredients:

- 60 ml honey
- 60 ml freshly squeezed lemon juice
- 2 tablespoons soy sauce
- 1 teaspoon garlic powder
- 1 (900 g) pork loin
- 2 tablespoons vegetable oil

Directions:

1. In a medium bowl, whisk together the honey, lemon juice, soy sauce, and garlic powder. Reserve half of the mixture for basting during cooking.
2. Cut 5 slits in the pork loin and transfer it to a resealable bag. Add the remaining honey mixture. Seal the bag and refrigerate to marinate for at least 2 hours.
3. Preheat the air fryer to 204°C. Line the two air fryer drawers with parchment paper.
4. Remove the pork from the marinade, and place it on the parchment. Spritz with oil, then baste with the reserved marinade.
5. Cook for 15 minutes. Flip the pork, baste with more marinade and spritz with oil again. Cook for 7 to 10 minutes more until the internal temperature reaches 64°C. Let rest for 5 minutes before serving.

Seasoned Lamb Steak

Servings: 2
Cooking Time: 10 Minutes
Ingredients:

- 2 lamb steaks
- ½ teaspoon kosher salt
- Drizzle of olive oil
- ½ teaspoon ground black pepper

Directions:

1. Take a bowl, add every ingredient except lamb steak. Mix well.
2. Rub lamb steaks with a little olive oil.
3. Press each side of steak into salt and pepper mixture.
4. Grease each basket of "Zone 1" and "Zone 2" of Tefal 2-Basket Air Fryer.
5. Press "Zone 1" and "Zone 2" and then rotate the knob for each zone to select "Air Fry".
6. Set the heat to 400 degrees F/ 200 degrees C for both zones and then set the time for 5 minutes to preheat.
7. After preheating, arrange steak into the basket of each zone.
8. Slide each basket into Air Fryer and set the time for 5 minutes.
9. While cooking, flip the steak once halfway through and cook for more 5 minutes.
10. After cooking time is completed, remove it from Air Fryer and place onto a platter for about 10 minutes before slicing.
11. With a sharp knife, cut each steak into desired-sized slices and serve.

Chinese Bbq Pork

Servings:35
Cooking Time:25
Ingredients:

- 4 tablespoons of soy sauce
- ¼ cup red wine
- 2 tablespoons of oyster sauce
- ¼ tablespoons of hoisin sauce
- ¼ cup honey
- ¼ cup brown sugar
- Pinch of salt
- Pinch of black pepper
- 1 teaspoon of ginger garlic, paste
- 1 teaspoon of five-spice powder
- 1.5 pounds of pork shoulder, sliced

Directions:

1. Take a bowl and mix all the ingredients listed under sauce ingredients.
2. Transfer half of it to a sauce pan and let it cook for 10 minutes.
3. Set it aside.
4. Let the pork marinate in the remaining sauce for 2 hours.
5. Afterward, put the pork slices in the basket and set it to AIRBORIL mode 450 degrees for 25 minutes.
6. Make sure the internal temperature is above 160 degrees F once cooked.
7. If not add a few more minutes to the overall cooking time.
8. Once done, take it out and baste it with prepared sauce.
9. Serve and Enjoy.

Nutrition:

- (Per serving) Calories 1239| Fat 73 g| Sodium 2185 mg | Carbs 57.3 g | Fiber 0.4g| Sugar53.7 g | Protein 81.5 g

Beef And Bean Taquitos With Mexican Rice

Servings:4
Cooking Time: 15 Minutes

Ingredients:

- FOR THE TAQUITOS
- ½ pound ground beef (85 percent lean)
- 1 tablespoon taco seasoning
- 8 (6-inch) soft white corn tortillas
- Nonstick cooking spray
- ¾ cup canned refried beans
- ½ cup shredded Mexican blend cheese (optional)
- FOR THE MEXICAN RICE
- 1 cup dried instant white rice (not microwavable)
- 1½ cups chicken broth
- ¼ cup jarred salsa
- 2 tablespoons canned tomato sauce
- 1 tablespoon vegetable oil
- ½ teaspoon kosher salt

Directions:

1. To prep the taquitos: In a large bowl, mix the ground beef and taco seasoning until well combined.

2. Mist both sides of each tortilla lightly with cooking spray.

3. To prep the Mexican rice: In the Zone 2 basket, combine the rice, broth, salsa, tomato sauce, oil, and salt. Stir well to ensure all of the rice is submerged in the liquid.

4. To cook the taquitos and rice: Install a crisper plate in the Zone 1 basket. Place the seasoned beef in the basket and insert the basket in the unit. Insert the Zone 2 basket in the unit.

5. Select Zone 1, select AIR FRY, set the temperature to 390°F, and set the time to 15 minutes.

6. Select Zone 2, select BAKE, set the temperature to 350°F, and set the time to 10 minutes. Select SMART FINISH.

7. Press START/PAUSE to begin cooking.

8. When the Zone 1 timer reads 10 minutes, press START/PAUSE. Remove the basket and transfer the beef to a medium bowl. Add the refried beans and cheese (if using) and combine well. Spoon 2 tablespoons of the filling onto each tortilla and roll tightly. Place the taquitos in the Zone 1 basket seam-side down. Reinsert the basket in the unit and press START/PAUSE to resume cooking.

9. When cooking is complete, the taquitos should be crisp and golden brown and the rice cooked through. Serve hot.

Nutrition:

- (Per serving) Calories: 431; Total fat: 18g; Saturated fat: 4g; Carbohydrates: 52g; Fiber: 5.5g; Protein: 18g; Sodium: 923mg

Italian Sausages With Peppers, Potatoes, And Onions

Servings:4
Cooking Time: 22 Minutes

Ingredients:

- FOR THE PEPPERS, POTATOES, AND ONIONS
- 2 Yukon Gold potatoes, cut into ¼-inch slices
- 1 red bell pepper, sliced
- 1 yellow onion, sliced
- ¼ cup canned tomato sauce
- 1 tablespoon olive oil
- 1 teaspoon minced garlic
- ½ teaspoon dried oregano
- ¼ teaspoon kosher salt
- FOR THE SAUSAGES
- 4 links Italian sausage

Directions:

1. To prep the peppers, potatoes, and onions: In a large bowl, combine the potatoes, pepper, onion, tomato sauce, oil, garlic, oregano, and salt. Mix to combine.

2. To cook the sausage and vegetables: Install a crisper plate in each of the two baskets. Place the sausages in the Zone 1 basket and insert the basket in the unit. Place the potato mixture in the Zone 2 basket and insert the basket in the unit.

3. Select Zone 1, select AIR FRY, set the temperature to 390°F, and set the time to 22 minutes.

4. Select Zone 2, select ROAST, set the temperature to 375°F, and set the time to 20 minutes. Select SMART FINISH.

5. Press START/PAUSE to begin cooking.

6. When cooking is complete, the sausages will be cooked through and the vegetables tender.

7. Slice the sausages into rounds, then mix them into the potato and pepper mixture. Serve.

Nutrition:

- (Per serving) Calories: 335; Total fat: 22g; Saturated fat: 6.5g; Carbohydrates: 21g; Fiber: 2g; Protein: 15g; Sodium: 658mg

Bacon-wrapped Hot Dogs With Mayo-ketchup Sauce

Servings: 5
Cooking Time: 10 To 12 Minutes
Ingredients:

- 10 thin slices of bacon
- 5 pork hot dogs, halved
- 1 teaspoon cayenne pepper
- Sauce:
- 60 ml mayonnaise
- 4 tablespoons ketchup
- 1 teaspoon rice vinegar
- 1 teaspoon chili powder

Directions:

1. Preheat the air fryer to 200ºC. 2. Arrange the slices of bacon on a clean work surface. One by one, place the halved hot dog on one end of each slice, season with cayenne pepper and wrap the hot dog with the bacon slices and secure with toothpicks as needed. 3. Place half the wrapped hot dogs in the two air fryer drawers and air fry for 10 to 12 minutes or until the bacon becomes browned and crispy. 4. Make the sauce: Stir all the ingredients for the sauce in a small bowl. Wrap the bowl in plastic and set in the refrigerator until ready to serve. 5. Transfer the hot dogs to a platter and serve hot with the sauce.

Blue Cheese Steak Salad

Servings: 4
Cooking Time: 22 Minutes
Ingredients:

- 2 tablespoons balsamic vinegar
- 2 tablespoons red wine vinegar
- 1 tablespoon Dijon mustard
- 1 tablespoon granulated sweetener
- 1 teaspoon minced garlic
- Sea salt and freshly ground black pepper, to taste
- 180 ml extra-virgin olive oil
- 450 g boneless rump steak
- Avocado oil spray
- 1 small red onion, cut into ¼-inch-thick rounds
- 170 g baby spinach
- 120 ml cherry tomatoes, halved
- 85 g blue cheese, crumbled

Directions:

1. In a blender, combine the balsamic vinegar, red wine vinegar, Dijon mustard, sweetener, and garlic. Season with salt and pepper and process until smooth. With the blender running, drizzle in the olive oil.

Process until well combined. Transfer to a jar with a tight-fitting lid, and refrigerate until ready to serve.

2. Season the steak with salt and pepper and let sit at room temperature for at least 45 minutes, time permitting.

3. Set the zone 1 air fryer drawer to 204ºC. Spray the steak with oil and place it in the zone 1 air fryer drawer. Spray the onion slices with oil and place them in the zone 2 air fryer drawer.

4. In zone 1, air fry for 6 minutes. Flip the steak and spray it with more oil. Air fry for 6 minutes more for medium-rare or until the steak is done to your liking.

5. In zone 2, cook at 204ºC for 5 minutes. Flip the onion slices and spray them with more oil. Air fry for 5 minutes more.

6. Transfer the steak to a plate, tent with a piece of aluminum foil, and allow it to rest. Slice the steak diagonally into thin strips. Place the spinach, cherry tomatoes, onion slices, and steak in a large bowl. Toss with the desired amount of dressing. Sprinkle with crumbled blue cheese and serve.

Goat Cheese-stuffed Bavette Steak

Servings: 6
Cooking Time: 14 Minutes
Ingredients:

- 450 g bavette or skirt steak
- 1 tablespoon avocado oil
- ½ teaspoon sea salt
- ½ teaspoon garlic powder
- ¼ teaspoon freshly ground black pepper
- 60 g goat cheese, crumbled
- 235 ml baby spinach, chopped

Directions:

1. Place the steak in a large zip-top bag or between two pieces of plastic wrap. Using a meat mallet or heavy-bottomed skillet, pound the steak to an even ¼-inch thickness.

2. Brush both sides of the steak with the avocado oil.

3. Mix the salt, garlic powder, and pepper in a small dish. Sprinkle this mixture over both sides of the steak.

4. Sprinkle the goat cheese over top, and top that with the spinach.

5. Starting at one of the long sides, roll the steak up tightly. Tie the rolled steak with kitchen string at 3-inch intervals.

6. Set the zone 1 air fryer drawer to 204ºC. Place the steak roll-up in the zone 1 air fryer drawer. Air fry for 7 minutes. Flip the steak and cook for an additional 7 minutes, until an instant-read thermometer reads 49ºC for medium-rare.

Tomahawk Steak

Servings: 4
Cooking Time: 12 Minutes
Ingredients:
- 4 tablespoons butter, softened
- 2 cloves garlic, minced
- 2 teaspoons chopped fresh parsley
- 1 teaspoon chopped chives
- 1 teaspoon chopped fresh thyme
- 1 teaspoon chopped fresh rosemary
- 2 (2 pounds each) bone-in ribeye steaks
- Kosher salt, to taste
- Freshly ground black pepper, to taste

Directions:
1. In a small bowl, combine the butter and herbs. Place the mixture in the center of a piece of plastic wrap and roll it into a log. Twist the ends together to keep it tight and refrigerate until hardened, about 20 minutes.
2. Season the steaks on both sides with salt and pepper.
3. Install a crisper plate in both drawers. Place one steak in the zone 1 drawer and one in zone 2's, then insert the drawers into the unit.
4. Select zone 1, select AIR FRY, set temperature to 390 degrees F/ 200 degrees C, and set time to 12 minutes. Select MATCH to match zone 2 settings to zone 1. Press the START/STOP button to begin cooking.
5. When the time reaches 10 minutes, press START/STOP to pause the unit. Remove the drawers and flip the steaks. Add the herb-butter to the tops of the steaks. Re-insert the drawers into the unit and press START/STOP to resume cooking.
6. Serve and enjoy!

Nutrition:
- (Per serving) Calories 338 | Fat 21.2g | Sodium 1503mg | Carbs 5.1g | Fiber 0.3g | Sugar 4.6g | Protein 29.3g

Juicy Pork Chops

Servings: 4
Cooking Time: 20 Minutes
Ingredients:
- 450g pork chops
- ¼ tsp garlic powder
- 15ml olive oil
- ¼ tsp smoked paprika
- Pepper
- Salt

Directions:
1. In a small bowl, mix the garlic powder, paprika, pepper, and salt.
2. Brush the pork chops with oil and rub with spice mixture.
3. Insert a crisper plate in the Tefal air fryer baskets.
4. Place the pork chops in both baskets.
5. Select zone 1, then select "bake" mode and set the temperature to 410 degrees F for 15 minutes. Press "match" to match zone 2 settings to zone 1. Press "start/stop" to begin. Turn halfway through.

Steak And Mashed Creamy Potatoes

Servings:1
Cooking Time:45
Ingredients:
- 2 Russet potatoes, peeled and cubed
- ¼ cup butter, divided
- 1/3 cup heavy cream
- ½ cup shredded cheddar cheese
- Salt and black pepper, to taste
- 1 New York strip steak, about a pound
- 1 teaspoon of olive oil
- Oil spray, for greasing

Directions:
1. Rub the potatoes with salt and a little amount of olive oil about a teaspoon.
2. Next, season the steak with salt and black pepper.
3. Place the russet potatoes in a zone 1 basket.
4. Oil spray the steak from both sides and then place it in the zone 2 basket.
5. Set zone 1 to AIR fry mode for 45 minutes at 390 degrees F.
6. Set the zone 2 basket, at 12 minutes at 375 degrees F.
7. Hot start and Lethe Tefal do its magic.
8. One the cooking cycle completes, take out the steak and potatoes.
9. Mash the potatoes and then add butter, heavy cream, and cheese along with salt and black pepper.
10. Serve the mashed potatoes with steak.
11. Enjoy.

Nutrition:
- (Per serving) Calories1932 | Fat 85.2g| Sodium 3069mg | Carbs 82g | Fiber10.3 g| Sugar 5.3g | Protein 22.5g

Cheesy Low-carb Lasagna

Servings: 4
Cooking Time: 10 Minutes
Ingredients:
- Meat Layer:
- Extra-virgin olive oil
- 450 g 85% lean beef mince
- 235 ml marinara sauce
- 60 ml diced celery
- 60 ml diced red onion
- ½ teaspoon minced garlic
- Coarse or flaky salt and black pepper, to taste
- Cheese Layer:
- 230 g ricotta cheese
- 235 ml shredded Mozzarella cheese
- 120 ml grated Parmesan cheese
- 2 large eggs
- 1 teaspoon dried Italian seasoning, crushed
- ½ teaspoon each minced garlic, garlic powder, and black pepper

Directions:
1. For the meat layer: Grease a cake pan with 1 teaspoon olive oil. 2. In a large bowl, combine the beef mince, marinara, celery, onion, garlic, salt, and pepper. Place the seasoned meat in the pan. 3. Place the pan in the zone 1 air fryer drawer. Set the temperature to 192ºC for 10 minutes. 4. Meanwhile, for the cheese layer: In a medium bowl, combine the ricotta, half the Mozzarella, the Parmesan, lightly beaten eggs, Italian seasoning, minced garlic, garlic powder, and pepper. Stir until well blended. 5. At the end of the cooking time, spread the cheese mixture over the meat mixture. Sprinkle with the remaining 120 ml Mozzarella. Set the temperature to 192ºC for 10 minutes, or until the cheese is browned and bubbling. 6. At the end of the cooking time, use a meat thermometer to ensure the meat has reached an internal temperature of 72ºC. 7. Drain the fat and liquid from the pan. Let stand for 5 minutes before serving.

Bacon-wrapped Vegetable Kebabs

Servings: 4
Cooking Time: 10 To 12 Minutes
Ingredients:
- 110 g mushrooms, sliced
- 1 small courgette, sliced
- 12 baby plum tomatoes
- 110 g sliced bacon, halved
- Avocado oil spray
- Sea salt and freshly ground black pepper, to taste

Directions:
1. Stack 3 mushroom slices, 1 courgette slice, and 1 tomato. Wrap a bacon strip around the vegetables and thread them onto a skewer. Repeat with the remaining vegetables and bacon. Spray with oil and sprinkle with salt and pepper.
2. Set the air fryer to 204ºC. Place the skewers in the two air fryer drawers in a single layer and air fry for 5 minutes. Flip the skewers and cook for 5 to 7 minutes more, until the bacon is crispy and the vegetables are tender.
3. Serve warm.

Sausage Meatballs

Servings: 24
Cooking Time: 30 Minutes
Ingredients:
- 1 egg, lightly beaten
- 900g pork sausage
- 29g breadcrumbs
- 100g pimientos, drained & diced
- 1 tsp curry powder
- 1 tbsp garlic, minced
- 30ml olive oil
- 1 tbsp fresh rosemary, minced
- 25g parsley, minced
- Pepper
- Salt

Directions:
1. In a bowl, add pork sausage and remaining ingredients and mix until well combined.
2. Insert a crisper plate in the Tefal air fryer baskets.
3. Make small balls from the meat mixture and place them in both baskets.
4. Select zone 1 then select "air fry" mode and set the temperature to 390 degrees F for 10 minutes. Press "match" to match zone 2 settings to zone 1. Press "start/stop" to begin.

Pork Chops With Brussels Sprouts

Servings: 4
Cooking Time: 15 Minutes.
Ingredients:
- 4 bone-in center-cut pork chop
- Cooking spray
- Salt, to taste
- Black pepper, to taste
- 2 teaspoons olive oil
- 2 teaspoons pure maple syrup
- 2 teaspoons Dijon mustard
- 6 ounces Brussels sprouts, quartered

Directions:
1. Rub pork chop with salt, ¼ teaspoons black pepper, and cooking spray.
2. Toss Brussels sprouts with mustard, syrup, oil, ¼ teaspoon of black pepper in a medium bowl.
3. Add pork chop to the crisper plate of Zone 1 of the Tefal Dual Zone Air Fryer.
4. Return the crisper plate to the Tefal Dual Zone Air Fryer.
5. Choose the Air Fry mode for Zone 1 and set the temperature to 400 degrees F and the time to 15 minutes.
6. Add the Brussels sprouts to the crisper plate of Zone 2 and return it to the unit.
7. Choose the Air Fry mode for Zone 2 with 350 degrees F and the time to 13 minutes.
8. Press the SYNC button to sync the finish time for both Zones.
9. Initiate cooking by pressing the START/STOP button.
10. Serve warm and fresh
Nutrition:
- (Per serving) Calories 336 | Fat 27.1g |Sodium 66mg | Carbs 1.1g | Fiber 0.4g | Sugar 0.2g | Protein 19.7g

Bo Luc Lac

Servings: 4
Cooking Time: 8 Minutes
Ingredients:
- For the Meat:
- 2 teaspoons soy sauce
- 4 garlic cloves, minced
- 1 teaspoon coarse or flaky salt
- 2 teaspoons sugar
- ¼ teaspoon ground black pepper
- 1 teaspoon toasted sesame oil
- 680 g top rump steak, cut into 1-inch cubes
- Cooking spray
- For the Salad:
- 1 head butterhead lettuce, leaves separated and torn into large pieces
- 60 ml fresh mint leaves
- 120 ml halved baby plum tomatoes
- ½ red onion, halved and thinly sliced
- 2 tablespoons apple cider vinegar
- 1 garlic clove, minced
- 2 teaspoons sugar
- ¼ teaspoon coarse or flaky salt
- ¼ teaspoon ground black pepper
- 2 tablespoons vegetable oil
- For Serving:
- Lime wedges, for garnish
- Coarse salt and freshly cracked black pepper, to taste

Directions:
1. Combine the ingredients for the meat, except for the steak, in a large bowl. Stir to mix well.
2. Dunk the steak cubes in the bowl and press to coat. Wrap the bowl in plastic and marinate under room temperature for at least 30 minutes.
3. Preheat the air fryer to 232°C. Spritz the two air fryer drawers with cooking spray.
4. Discard the marinade and transfer the steak cubes in the two preheated air fryer drawers.
5. Air fry for 4 minutes or until the steak cubes are lightly browned but still have a little pink. Shake the drawers halfway through the cooking time.
6. Meanwhile, combine the ingredients for the salad in a separate large bowl. Toss to mix well.
7. Pour the salad in a large serving bowl and top with the steak cubes. Squeeze the lime wedges over and sprinkle with salt and black pepper before serving.

Roast Beef

Servings: 4
Cooking Time: 35 Minutes
Ingredients:

- 2 pounds beef roast
- 1 tablespoon olive oil
- 1 medium onion (optional)
- 1 teaspoon salt
- 2 teaspoons rosemary and thyme, chopped (fresh or dried)

Directions:

1. Combine the sea salt, rosemary, and oil in a large, shallow dish.
2. Using paper towels, pat the meat dry. Place it on a dish and turn it to coat the outside with the oil-herb mixture.
3. Peel the onion and split it in half (if using).
4. Install a crisper plate in both drawers. Place half the beef roast and half an onion in the zone 1 drawer and half the beef and half the onion in zone 2's, then insert the drawers into the unit.
5. Select zone 1, select AIR FRY, set temperature to 360 degrees F/ 180 degrees C, and set time to 22 minutes. Select MATCH to match zone 2 settings to zone 1. Press the START/STOP button to begin cooking.
6. When the time reaches 11 minutes, press START/STOP to pause the unit. Remove the drawers and flip the roast. Re-insert the drawers into the unit and press START/STOP to resume cooking.

Nutrition:

- (Per serving) Calories 463 | Fat 17.8g | Sodium 732mg | Carbs 2.8g | Fiber 0.7g | Sugar 1.2g | Protein 69g

Parmesan Pork Chops

Servings: 4
Cooking Time: 15 Minutes.
Ingredients:

- 4 boneless pork chops
- 2 tablespoons olive oil
- ½ cup freshly grated Parmesan
- 1 teaspoon salt
- 1 teaspoon paprika
- 1 teaspoon garlic powder
- 1 teaspoon onion powder
- ½ teaspoon black pepper

Directions:

1. Pat dry the pork chops with a paper towel and rub them with olive oil.

2. Mix parmesan with spices in a medium bowl.
3. Rub the pork chops with Parmesan mixture.
4. Place 2 seasoned pork chops in each of the two crisper plate
5. Return the crisper plate to the Tefal Dual Zone Air Fryer.
6. Choose the Air Fry mode for Zone 1 and set the temperature to 390 degrees F and the time to 15 minutes.
7. Select the "MATCH" button to copy the settings for Zone 2.
8. Initiate cooking by pressing the START/STOP button.
9. Flip the pork chops when cooked halfway through, then resume cooking.
10. Serve warm.

Nutrition:

- (Per serving) Calories 396 | Fat 23.2g |Sodium 622mg | Carbs 0.7g | Fiber 0g | Sugar 0g | Protein 45.6g

Garlic Sirloin Steak

Servings: 4
Cooking Time: 10 Minutes
Ingredients:

- 4 sirloin steak
- 30ml olive oil
- 28g steak sauce
- ½ tsp ground coriander
- 1 tsp garlic, minced
- 1 tbsp thyme, chopped
- Pepper
- Salt

Directions:

1. In a bowl, mix steak with thyme, oil, steak sauce, coriander, garlic, pepper, and salt. Cover and set aside for 2 hours.
2. Insert a crisper plate in Tefal air fryer baskets.
3. Place the marinated steaks in both baskets.
4. Select zone 1 then select air fry mode and set the temperature to 360 degrees F for 10 minutes. Press "match" and then "start/stop" to begin.

Mozzarella Stuffed Beef And Pork Meatballs

Servings: 4 To 6
Cooking Time: 12 Minutes
Ingredients:

- 1 tablespoon olive oil
- 1 small onion, finely chopped
- 1 to 2 cloves garlic, minced
- 340 g beef mince
- 340 g pork mince
- 180 ml bread crumbs
- 60 ml grated Parmesan cheese
- 60 ml finely chopped fresh parsley
- ½ teaspoon dried oregano
- 1½ teaspoons salt
- Freshly ground black pepper, to taste
- 2 eggs, lightly beaten
- 140 g low-moisture Mozzarella or other melting cheese, cut into 1-inch cubes

Directions:

1. Preheat a skillet over medium-high heat. Add the oil and cook the onion and garlic until tender, but not browned. 2. Transfer the onion and garlic to a large bowl and add the beef, pork, bread crumbs, Parmesan cheese, parsley, oregano, salt, pepper and eggs. Mix well until all the ingredients are combined. Divide the mixture into 12 evenly sized balls. Make one meatball at a time, by pressing a hole in the meatball mixture with the finger and pushing a piece of Mozzarella cheese into the hole. Mold the meat back into a ball, enclosing the cheese. 3. Preheat the air fryer to 192°C. 4. Transfer meatballs to the two air fryer drawers and air fry for 12 minutes, shaking the drawers and turning the meatballs twice during the cooking process. Serve warm.

Italian Sausages With Peppers And Teriyaki Rump Steak With Broccoli

Servings: 7
Cooking Time: 28 Minutes
Ingredients:

- Italian Sausages with Peppers:
- 1 medium onion, thinly sliced
- 1 yellow or orange pepper, thinly sliced
- 1 red pepper, thinly sliced
- 60 ml avocado oil or melted coconut oil
- 1 teaspoon fine sea salt
- 6 Italian-seasoned sausages
- Dijon mustard, for serving (optional)
- Teriyaki Rump Steak with Broccoli:
- 230 g rump steak
- 80 ml teriyaki marinade
- 1½ teaspoons sesame oil
- ½ head broccoli, cut into florets
- 2 red peppers, sliced
- Fine sea salt and ground black pepper, to taste
- Cooking spray

Directions:

1. Make the Italian Sausages with Peppers :
2. Preheat the air fryer to 204°C.
3. Place the onion and peppers in a large bowl. Drizzle with the oil and toss well to coat the veggies. Season with the salt.
4. Place the onion and peppers in a pie pan and cook in the air fryer for 8 minutes, stirring halfway through. Remove from the air fryer and set aside.
5. Spray the zone 1 air fryer drawer with avocado oil. Place the sausages in the zone 1 air fryer drawer and air fry for 20 minutes, or until crispy and golden brown. During the last minute or two of cooking, add the onion and peppers to the drawer with the sausages to warm them through.
6. Place the onion and peppers on a serving platter and arrange the sausages on top. Serve Dijon mustard on the side, if desired.
7. Store leftovers in an airtight container in the fridge for up to 7 days or in the freezer for up to a month. Reheat in a preheated 200°C air fryer for 3 minutes, or until heated through.
8. Make the Teriyaki Rump Steak with Broccoli :
9. Toss the rump steak in a large bowl with teriyaki marinade. Wrap the bowl in plastic and refrigerate to marinate for at least an hour.
10. Preheat the air fryer to 204°C and spritz with cooking spray.
11. Discard the marinade and transfer the steak in the preheated zone 2 air fryer drawer. Spritz with cooking spray.
12. Air fry for 13 minutes or until well browned. Flip the steak halfway through.
13. Meanwhile, heat the sesame oil in a nonstick skillet over medium heat. Add the broccoli and red pepper. Sprinkle with salt and ground black pepper. Sauté for 5 minutes or until the broccoli is tender.
14. Transfer the air fried rump steak on a plate and top with the sautéed broccoli and pepper. Serve hot.

Steak Fajitas With Onions And Peppers

Servings: 6
Cooking Time: 15 Minutes
Ingredients:

- 1 pound steak
- 1 green bell pepper, sliced
- 1 yellow bell pepper, sliced
- 1 red bell pepper, sliced
- ½ cup sliced white onions
- 1 packet gluten-free fajita seasoning
- Olive oil spray

Directions:

1. Thinly slice the steak against the grain. These should be about ¼-inch slices.
2. Mix the steak with the peppers and onions.
3. Evenly coat with the fajita seasoning.
4. Install a crisper plate in both drawers. Place half the steak mixture in the zone 1 drawer and half in zone 2's, then insert the drawers into the unit.
5. Select zone 1, select AIR FRY, set temperature to 390 degrees F/ 200 degrees C, and set time to 15 minutes. Select MATCH to match zone 2 settings to zone 1. Press the START/STOP button to begin cooking.
6. When the time reaches 10 minutes, press START/STOP to pause the unit. Remove the drawers and flip the steak strips. Re-insert the drawers into the unit and press START/STOP to resume cooking.
7. Serve in warm tortillas.

Nutrition:

- (Per serving) Calories 305 | Fat 17g | Sodium 418mg | Carbs 15g | Fiber 2g | Sugar 4g | Protein 22g

Mustard Pork Chops

Servings: 4
Cooking Time: 15 Minutes
Ingredients:

- 450g pork chops, boneless
- 55g brown mustard
- 85g honey
- 57g mayonnaise
- 34g BBQ sauce
- Pepper
- Salt

Directions:

1. Coat pork chops with mustard, honey, mayonnaise, BBQ sauce, pepper, and salt in a bowl. Cover and place the bowl in the refrigerator for 1 hour.

2. Insert a crisper plate in the Tefal air fryer baskets.
3. Place the marinated pork chops in both baskets.
4. Select zone 1, then select "bake" mode and set the temperature to 380 degrees F for 15 minutes. Press "match" and then press "start/stop" to begin. Turn halfway through.

Beef Kofta Kebab

Servings: 4
Cooking Time: 20 Minutes
Ingredients:

- 455g ground beef
- ¼ cup white onion, grated
- ¼ cup parsley, chopped
- 1 tablespoon mint, chopped
- 2 cloves garlic, minced
- 1 teaspoon salt
- ½ teaspoon cumin
- 1 teaspoon oregano
- ½ teaspoon garlic salt
- 1 egg

Directions:

1. Mix ground beef with onion, parsley, mint, garlic, cumin, oregano, garlic salt and egg in a bowl.
2. Take 3 tbsp-sized beef kebabs out of this mixture.
3. Place the kebabs in the air fryer baskets.
4. Return the air fryer basket 1 to Zone 1, and basket 2 to Zone 2 of the Tefal 2-Basket Air Fryer.
5. Choose the "Air Fry" mode for Zone 1 at 375 degrees F and 18 minutes of cooking time.
6. Select the "MATCH COOK" option to copy the settings for Zone 2.
7. Initiate cooking by pressing the START/PAUSE BUTTON.
8. Flip the kebabs once cooked halfway through.

Cheeseburgers With Barbecue Potato Chips

Servings:4

Cooking Time: 15 Minutes

Ingredients:

- FOR THE CHEESEBURGERS
- 1 pound ground beef (85 percent lean)
- ¼ teaspoon kosher salt
- ¼ teaspoon freshly ground black pepper
- ½ teaspoon olive oil
- 4 slices American cheese
- 4 hamburger rolls
- FOR THE POTATO CHIPS
- 2 large russet potatoes
- 2 teaspoons vegetable oil
- 1½ teaspoons smoked paprika
- 1 teaspoon light brown sugar
- ½ teaspoon garlic powder
- ½ teaspoon kosher salt
- ¼ teaspoon chili powder

Directions:

1. To prep the cheeseburgers: Season the beef with the salt and black pepper. Form the beef into 4 patties about 1 inch thick. Brush both sides of the beef patties with the oil.

2. To prep the potato chips: Fill a large bowl with ice water. Using a mandoline or sharp knife, cut the potatoes into very thin (⅛- to 1/16-inch) slices. Soak the potatoes in the ice water for 30 minutes.

3. Drain the potatoes and pat dry with a paper towel. Place in a large bowl and toss with the oil, smoked paprika, brown sugar, garlic powder, salt, and chili powder.

4. To cook the cheeseburgers and potato chips: Install a crisper plate in each of the two baskets. Place the burgers in the Zone 1 basket and insert the basket in the unit. Place the potato slices in the Zone 2 basket and insert the basket in the unit.

5. Select Zone 1, select AIR FRY, set the temperature to 390°F, and set the time to 12 minutes.

6. Select Zone 2, select AIR FRY, set the temperature to 390°F, and set the time to 15 minutes. Select SMART FINISH.

7. Press START/PAUSE to begin cooking.

8. At 5-minute intervals, press START/PAUSE. Remove the Zone 2 basket and shake the potato chips to keep them from sticking to each other. Reinsert the basket and press START/PAUSE to resume cooking.

9. When cooking is complete, the burgers should be cooked to your preferred doneness and the potato chips should be crisp and golden brown.

10. Top each burger patty in the basket with a slice of cheese. Turn the air fryer off and let the cheese melt inside the unit, or cover the basket with aluminum foil and let stand for 1 to 2 minutes, until the cheese is melted. Serve the cheeseburgers on buns with the chips on the side.

Nutrition:

- (Per serving) Calories: 475; Total fat: 22g; Saturated fat: 8g; Carbohydrates: 38g; Fiber: 2g; Protein: 32g; Sodium: 733mg

11. Serve warm.

Chicken Caprese

Servings: 4
Cooking Time: 10 Minutes
Ingredients:
- 4 chicken breast cutlets
- 1 teaspoon Italian seasoning
- 1 teaspoon salt
- ½ teaspoon black pepper
- 4 slices fresh mozzarella cheese
- 1 large tomato, sliced
- Basil and balsamic vinegar to garnish

Directions:
1. Pat dry the chicken cutlets with a kitchen towel.
2. Rub the chicken with Italian seasoning, black pepper and salt.
3. Place two chicken breasts in each air fryer basket.
4. Return the air fryer basket 1 to Zone 1, and basket 2 to Zone 2 of the Tefal 2-Basket Air Fryer.
5. Choose the "Air Fry" mode for Zone 1 at 375 degrees F and 10 minutes of cooking time.
6. Select the "MATCH COOK" option to copy the settings for Zone 2.
7. Initiate cooking by pressing the START/PAUSE BUTTON.
8. After 10 minutes top each chicken breast with a slice of cheese and tomato slices.
9. Return the baskets to the Tefal 2 Baskets Air Fryer and air fry for 5 another minutes.
10. Garnish with balsamic vinegar and basil.
11. Serve warm.

Nutrition:
- (Per serving) Calories 502 | Fat 25g |Sodium 230mg | Carbs 1.5g | Fiber 0.2g | Sugar 0.4g | Protein 64.1g

Lemon Thyme Roasted Chicken

Servings: 6
Cooking Time: 60 Minutes
Ingredients:
- 2 tablespoons baking powder
- 1 teaspoon smoked paprika
- Sea salt and freshly ground black pepper, to taste
- 900 g chicken wings or chicken drumettes
- Avocado oil spray
- 80 ml avocado oil
- 120 ml Buffalo hot sauce, such as Frank's RedHot
- 4 tablespoons unsalted butter
- 2 tablespoons apple cider vinegar
- 1 teaspoon minced garlic

Directions:
1. In a large bowl, stir together the baking powder, smoked paprika, and salt and pepper to taste. Add the chicken wings and toss to coat.
2. Set the air fryer to 200°C. Spray the wings with oil.
3. Place the wings in the two drawers in a single layer and air fry for 20 to 25 minutes. Check with an instant-read thermometer and remove when they reach 70°C. Let rest until they reach 76°C.
4. While the wings are cooking, whisk together the avocado oil, hot sauce, butter, vinegar, and garlic in a small saucepan over medium-low heat until warm.
5. When the wings are done cooking, toss them with the Buffalo sauce. Serve warm.

Easy Cajun Chicken Drumsticks

Servings: 5
Cooking Time: 40 Minutes
Ingredients:
- 1 tablespoon olive oil
- 10 chicken drumsticks
- 1½ tablespoons Cajun seasoning
- Salt and ground black pepper, to taste

Directions:
1. Preheat the air fryer to 200°C. Grease the two air fryer drawers with olive oil. 2. On a clean work surface, rub the chicken drumsticks with Cajun seasoning, salt, and ground black pepper. 3. Arrange the seasoned chicken drumsticks in a single layer in the air fryer. 4. Air fry for 18 minutes or until lightly browned. Flip the drumsticks halfway through. 5. Remove the chicken drumsticks from the air fryer. Serve immediately.

Spice-rubbed Chicken Pieces

Servings:6
Cooking Time:40
Ingredients:

- 3 pounds chicken, pieces
- 1 teaspoon sweet paprika
- 1 teaspoon mustard powder
- 1 tablespoon brown sugar, dark
- Salt and black pepper, to taste
- 1 teaspoon Chile powder, New Mexico
- 1 teaspoon oregano, dried
- ¼ teaspoon allspice powder, ground

Directions:

1. Take a bowl and mix dark brown sugar, salt, paprika, mustard powder, oregano, Chile powder, black pepper, and all spice powder.
2. Mix well and rub this spice mixture all over the chicken.
3. Divide the chicken between two air fryer baskets.
4. Oil sprays the meat and then adds it to the air fryer.
5. Now press button1 and button 2 and set the time to 40 minutes at 350 degrees F.
6. Now press start and once the cooking cycle completes, press pause for both the zones.
7. Take out the chicken and serve hot.

Nutrition:

- (Per serving) Calories353 | Fat 7.1g| Sodium400 mg | Carbs 2.2g | Fiber0.4 g | Sugar 1.6g | Protein66 g

Fajita Chicken Strips & Barbecued Chicken With Creamy Coleslaw

Servings: 6
Cooking Time: 20 Minutes
Ingredients:

- Fajita Chicken Strips:
- 450 g boneless, skinless chicken tenderloins, cut into strips
- 3 bell peppers, any color, cut into chunks
- 1 onion, cut into chunks
- 1 tablespoon olive oil
- 1 tablespoon fajita seasoning mix
- Cooking spray
- Barbecued Chicken with Creamy Coleslaw:
- 270 g shredded coleslaw mix
- Salt and pepper
- 2 (340 g) bone-in split chicken breasts, trimmed
- 1 teaspoon vegetable oil
- 2 tablespoons barbecue sauce, plus extra for serving
- 2 tablespoons mayonnaise
- 2 tablespoons sour cream
- 1 teaspoon distilled white vinegar, plus extra for seasoning
- ¼ teaspoon sugar

Directions:

1. Make the Fajita Chicken Strips :
2. Preheat the air fryer to 190°C.
3. In a large bowl, mix together the chicken, bell peppers, onion, olive oil, and fajita seasoning mix until completely coated.
4. Spray the zone 1 air fryer basket lightly with cooking spray.
5. Place the chicken and vegetables in the zone 1 air fryer basket and lightly spray with cooking spray.
6. Air fry for 7 minutes. Shake the basket and air fry for an additional 5 to 8 minutes, until the chicken is cooked through and the veggies are starting to char.
7. Serve warm.
8. Make the Barbecued Chicken with Creamy Coleslaw :
9. Preheat the air fryer to 180°C.
10. Toss coleslaw mix and ¼ teaspoon salt in a colander set over bowl. Let sit until wilted slightly, about 30 minutes. Rinse, drain, and dry well with a dish towel.
11. Meanwhile, pat chicken dry with paper towels, rub with oil, and season with salt and pepper. Arrange breasts skin-side down in zone 2 air fryer basket, spaced evenly apart, alternating ends. Bake for 10 minutes. Flip breasts and brush skin side with barbecue sauce. Return basket to air fryer and bake until well browned and chicken registers 70°C, 10 to 15 minutes.
12. Transfer chicken to serving platter, tent loosely with aluminum foil, and let rest for 5 minutes. While chicken rests, whisk mayonnaise, sour cream, vinegar, sugar, and pinch pepper together in a large bowl. Stir in coleslaw mix and season with salt, pepper, and additional vinegar to taste. Serve chicken with coleslaw, passing extra barbecue sauce separately.

Chicken Parmesan With Roasted Lemon-parmesan Broccoli

Servings: 4
Cooking Time: 18 Minutes
Ingredients:
- FOR THE CHICKEN PARMESAN
- 2 tablespoons all-purpose flour
- 2 large eggs
- 1 cup panko bread crumbs
- 2 tablespoons grated Parmesan cheese
- 2 teaspoons Italian seasoning
- 4 thin-sliced chicken cutlets (4 ounces each)
- 2 tablespoons vegetable oil
- ½ cup marinara sauce
- ½ cup shredded part-skim mozzarella cheese
- FOR THE BROCCOLI
- 4 cups broccoli florets
- 2 tablespoons olive oil, divided
- ¼ teaspoon kosher salt
- ¼ teaspoon freshly ground black pepper
- 2 teaspoons fresh lemon juice
- 2 tablespoons grated Parmesan cheese

Directions:
1. To prep the chicken Parmesan:
2. Set up a breading station with 3 small shallow bowls. Place the flour in the first bowl. In the second bowl, beat the eggs. Combine the panko, Parmesan, and Italian seasoning in the third bowl.
3. Bread the chicken cutlets in this order: First, dip them into the flour, coating both sides. Then, dip into the beaten egg. Finally, place in the panko mixture, coating both sides of the cutlets. Drizzle the oil over the cutlets.
4. To prep the broccoli: In a large bowl, combine the broccoli, 1 tablespoon of olive oil, the salt, and black pepper.
5. To cook the chicken and broccoli:
6. Install a crisper plate in the Zone 1 basket. Place the chicken in the basket and insert the basket in the unit. Place the broccoli in the Zone 2 basket and insert the basket in the unit.
7. Select Zone 1, select AIR FRY, set the temperature to 390°F, and set the time to 18 minutes.
8. Select Zone 2, select ROAST, set the temperature to 390°F, and set the time to 15 minutes. Select SMART FINISH.
9. Press START/PAUSE to begin cooking.
10. When the Zone 1 timer reads 10 minutes, press START/PAUSE. Remove the basket and use silicone-tipped tongs to flip the chicken. Reinsert the basket and press START/PAUSE to resume cooking.
11. When the Zone 1 timer reads 2 minutes, press START/PAUSE. Remove the basket and spoon 2 tablespoons of marinara sauce over each chicken cutlet. Sprinkle the mozzarella on top. Reinsert the basket and press START/PAUSE to resume cooking.
12. When cooking is complete, the cheese will be melted and the chicken cooked through . Transfer the broccoli to a large bowl. Add the lemon juice and Parmesan and toss to coat. Serve the chicken and broccoli warm.

Buffalo Chicken

Servings: 4
Cooking Time: 22 Minutes
Ingredients:
- ½ cup plain fat-free Greek yogurt
- ¼ cup egg substitute
- 1 tablespoon plus 1 teaspoon hot sauce
- 1 cup panko breadcrumbs
- 1 tablespoon sweet paprika
- 1 tablespoon garlic pepper seasoning
- 1 tablespoon cayenne pepper
- 1-pound skinless, boneless chicken breasts, cut into 1-inch strips

Directions:
1. Combine the Greek yogurt, egg substitute, and hot sauce in a mixing bowl.
2. In a separate bowl, combine the panko breadcrumbs, paprika, garlic powder, and cayenne pepper.
3. Dip the chicken strips in the yogurt mixture, then coat them in the breadcrumb mixture.
4. Install a crisper plate in both drawers. Place the chicken strips into the drawers and then insert the drawers into the unit.
5. Select zone 1, select AIR FRY, set temperature to 390 degrees F/ 200 degrees C, and set time to 22 minutes. Select MATCH to match zone 2 settings to zone 1. Press the START/STOP button to begin cooking.
6. When cooking is complete, serve immediately.

Nutrition:
- (Per serving) Calories 234 | Fat 15.8g | Sodium 696mg | Carbs 22.1g | Fiber 1.1g | Sugar 1.7g | Protein 31.2g

Cracked-pepper Chicken Wings

Servings: 4
Cooking Time: 20 Minutes
Ingredients:
- 450 g chicken wings
- 3 tablespoons vegetable oil
- 60 g all-purpose flour
- ½ teaspoon smoked paprika
- ½ teaspoon garlic powder
- ½ teaspoon kosher salt
- 1½ teaspoons freshly cracked black pepper

Directions:
1. Place the chicken wings in a large bowl. Drizzle the vegetable oil over wings and toss to coat.
2. In a separate bowl, whisk together the flour, paprika, garlic powder, salt, and pepper until combined.
3. Dredge the wings in the flour mixture one at a time, coating them well, and place in the zone 1 air fryer drawer. Set the temperature to 200°C for 20 minutes, turning the wings halfway through the cooking time, until the breading is browned and crunchy.

Yummy Chicken Breasts

Servings:2
Cooking Time:25
Ingredients:
- 4 large chicken breasts, 6 ounces each
- 2 tablespoons of oil bay seasoning
- 1 tablespoon Montreal chicken seasoning
- 1 teaspoon of thyme
- 1/2 teaspoon of paprika
- Salt, to taste
- oil spray, for greasing

Directions:
1. Season the chicken breast pieces with the listed seasoning and let them rest for 40 minutes.
2. Grease both sides of the chicken breast pieces with oil spray.
3. Divide the chicken breast piece between both baskets.
4. Set zone 1 to AIRFRY mode at 400 degrees F, for 15 minutes.
5. Select the MATCH button for another basket.
6. Select pause and take out the baskets and flip the chicken breast pieces, after 15 minutes.

7. Select the zones to 400 degrees F for 10 more minutes using the MATCH cook button.
8. Once it's done serve.
Nutrition:
- (Per serving) Calories 711| Fat 27.7g| Sodium 895mg | Carbs 1.6g | Fiber 0.4g | Sugar 0.1g | Protein 106.3g

Chicken Bites

Servings: 4
Cooking Time: 20 Minutes
Ingredients:
- 900g chicken thighs, cut into chunks
- ¼ tsp white pepper
- ½ tsp onion powder
- 30ml olive oil
- 59ml fresh lemon juice
- ½ tsp garlic powder
- Pepper
- Salt

Directions:
1. Add chicken chunks and remaining ingredients into the bowl and mix well.
2. Cover the bowl and place it in the refrigerator overnight.
3. Insert a crisper plate in the Tefal air fryer baskets.
4. Place the marinated chicken in both baskets.
5. Select zone 1 then select "air fry" mode and set the temperature to 380 degrees F for 20 minutes. Press "match" to match zone 2 settings to zone 1. Press "start/stop" to begin.
Nutrition:
- (Per serving) Calories 497 | Fat 23.9g |Sodium 237mg | Carbs 0.9g | Fiber 0.2g | Sugar 0.5g | Protein 65.8g

Apricot-glazed Turkey Tenderloin

Servings: 4
Cooking Time: 30 Minutes
Ingredients:
- Olive oil
- 80 g sugar-free apricot preserves
- ½ tablespoon spicy brown mustard
- 680 g turkey breast tenderloin
- Salt and freshly ground black pepper, to taste

Directions:
1. Spray the two air fryer drawers lightly with olive oil.
2. In a small bowl, combine the apricot preserves and mustard to make a paste.
3. Season the turkey with salt and pepper. Spread the apricot paste all over the turkey.
4. Place the turkey in the two air fryer drawers and lightly spray with olive oil.
5. Air fry at 190°C for 15 minutes. Flip the turkey over and lightly spray with olive oil. Air fry until the internal temperature reaches at least 80°C, an additional 10 to 15 minutes.
6. Let the turkey rest for 10 minutes before slicing and serving.

Bbq Cheddar-stuffed Chicken Breasts

Servings: 2
Cooking Time: 25 Minutes
Ingredients:
- 3 strips cooked bacon, divided
- 2 ounces cheddar cheese, cubed, divided
- ¼ cup BBQ sauce, divided
- 2 (4-ounces) skinless, boneless chicken breasts
- Salt and ground black pepper, to taste

Directions:
1. In a mixing bowl, combine the cooked bacon, cheddar cheese, and 1 tablespoon BBQ sauce.
2. Make a horizontal 1-inch cut at the top of each chicken breast with a long, sharp knife, producing a little interior pouch. Fill each breast with an equal amount of the bacon-cheese mixture. Wrap the remaining bacon strips around each chicken breast. Coat the chicken breasts with the leftover BBQ sauce and lay them in a baking dish.
3. Install a crisper plate in both drawers. Place half the chicken breasts in zone 1 and half in zone 2, then insert the drawers into the unit.

4. Select zone 1, select AIR FRY, set temperature to 390 degrees F/ 200 degrees C, and set time to 22 minutes. Select MATCH to match zone 2 settings to zone 1. Press the START/STOP button to begin cooking.
5. When the time reaches 11 minutes, press START/STOP to pause the unit. Remove the drawers and flip the chicken. Re-insert drawers into the unit and press START/STOP to resume cooking.
6. When cooking is complete, remove the chicken breasts.

Nutrition:
- (Per serving) Calories 379 | Fat 12.8g | Sodium 906mg | Carbs 11.1g | Fiber 0.4g | Sugar 8.3g | Protein 37.7g

Spiced Chicken And Vegetables

Servings:1
Cooking Time:45
Ingredients:
- 2 large chicken breasts
- 2 teaspoons of olive oil
- 1 teaspoon of chili powder
- 1 teaspoon of paprika powder
- 1 teaspoon of onion powder
- ½ teaspoon of garlic powder
- 1/4 teaspoon of Cumin
- Salt and black pepper, to taste
- Vegetable Ingredients:
- 2 large potato, cubed
- 4 large carrots cut into bite-size pieces
- 1 tablespoon of olive oil
- Salt and black pepper, to taste

Directions:
1. Take chicken breast pieces and rub olive oil, salt, pepper, chili powder, onion powder, cumin, garlic powder, and paprika.
2. Season the vegetables with olive oil, salt, and black pepper.
3. Now put the chicken breast pieces in the zone 1 basket.
4. Put the vegetables into the zone 2 basket.
5. Now hit 1 for the first basket and set it to ROAST at 350 degrees F, for 45 minutes.
6. For the second basket hit 2 and set time for 45 minutes, by selecting AIR FRY mode at 350 degrees F.
7. To start cooking hit the smart finish button and press hit start.
8. Once the cooking cycle is done, serve, and enjoy.

Nutrition:
- (Per serving) Calories1510 | Fat 51.3g| Sodium 525mg | Carbs 163g | Fiber24.7 g | Sugar 21.4g | Protein 102.9

Chicken Potatoes

Servings: 4
Cooking Time: 22 Minutes
Ingredients:
- 15 ounces canned potatoes drained
- 1 teaspoon olive oil
- 1 teaspoon Lawry's seasoned salt
- ⅛ teaspoons black pepper optional
- 8 ounces boneless chicken breast cubed
- ¼ teaspoon paprika
- ⅜ cup cheddar, shredded
- 4 bacon slices, cooked, cut into strips

Directions:
1. Dice the chicken into small pieces and toss them with olive oil and spices.
2. Drain and dice the potato pieces into smaller cubes.
3. Add potato to the chicken and mix well to coat.
4. Spread the mixture in the two crisper plates in a single layer.
5. Return the crisper plates to the Tefal Dual Zone Air Fryer.
6. Choose the Air Fry mode for Zone 1 and set the temperature to 390 degrees F and the time to 22 minutes|
7. Select the "MATCH" button to copy the settings for Zone 2.
8. Initiate cooking by pressing the START/STOP button.
9. Top the chicken and potatoes with cheese and bacon.
10. Return the crisper plates to the Tefal Dual Zone Air Fryer.
11. Select the Max Crisp mode for Zone 1 and set the temperature to 300 degrees F and the time to 5 minutes|
12. Initiate cooking by pressing the START/STOP button.
13. Repeat the same step for Zone 2 to broil the potatoes and chicken in the right drawer.
14. Enjoy with dried herbs on top.

Garlic Parmesan Drumsticks

Servings: 4
Cooking Time: 25 Minutes
Ingredients:
- 8 (115 g) chicken drumsticks
- ½ teaspoon salt
- ⅛ teaspoon ground black pepper
- ½ teaspoon garlic powder
- 2 tablespoons salted butter, melted
- 45 g grated Parmesan cheese
- 1 tablespoon dried parsley

Directions:
1. Sprinkle drumsticks with salt, pepper, and garlic powder. Place drumsticks into the two ungreased air fryer baskets.
2. Adjust the temperature to 200ºC and air fry for 25 minutes, turning drumsticks halfway through cooking. Drumsticks will be golden and have an internal temperature of at least 75ºC when done.
3. Transfer drumsticks to a large serving dish. Pour butter over drumsticks, and sprinkle with Parmesan and parsley. Serve warm.

Spicy Chicken

Servings:40
Cooking Time:35
Ingredients:
- 4 chicken thighs
- 2 cups of butter milk
- 4 chicken legs
- 2 cups of flour
- Salt and black pepper, to taste
- 2 tablespoons garlic powder
- ½ teaspoon onion powder
- 1 teaspoon poultry seasoning
- 1 teaspoon cumin
- 2 tablespoons paprika
- 1 tablespoon olive oil

Directions:
1. Take a bowl and add buttermilk to it.
2. Soak the chicken thighs and chicken legs in the buttermilk for 2 hours.
3. Mix flour, all the seasonings, and olive oil in a small bowl.
4. Take out the chicken pieces from the buttermilk mixture and then dredge them into the flour mixture.
5. Repeat the steps for all the pieces and then arrange them into both the air fryer basket.
6. Set the timer for both the basket by selecting a roast mode for 35-40 minutes at 350 degrees F.
7. Once the cooking cycle complete select the pause button and then take out the basket.
8. Serve and enjoy.
Nutrition:
- (Per serving) Calories 624| Fat17.6 g| Sodium300 mg | Carbs 60g | Fiber 3.5g | Sugar 7.7g | Protein54.2 g

Coconut Chicken Tenders With Broiled Utica Greens

Servings: 4
Cooking Time: 25 Minutes
Ingredients:
- FOR THE CHICKEN TENDERS
- 2 tablespoons all-purpose flour
- 2 large eggs
- 1 cup unsweetened shredded coconut
- ¾ cup panko bread crumbs
- ½ teaspoon kosher salt
- 1½ pounds chicken tenders
- Nonstick cooking spray
- FOR THE UTICA GREENS
- 12 ounces frozen chopped escarole or Swiss chard, thawed and drained
- ¼ cup diced prosciutto
- 2 tablespoons chopped pickled cherry peppers
- ½ teaspoon garlic powder
- ½ teaspoon onion powder
- ¼ teaspoon kosher salt
- ¼ cup Italian-style bread crumbs
- ¼ cup grated Romano cheese
- Nonstick cooking spray

Directions:
1. To prep the chicken tenders:
2. Set up a breading station with three small shallow bowls. Place the flour in the first bowl. In the second bowl, beat the eggs. Combine the coconut, bread crumbs, and salt in the third bowl.
3. Bread the chicken tenders in this order: First, coat them in the flour. Then, dip into the beaten egg. Finally, coat them in the coconut breading, gently pressing the breading into the chicken to help it adhere. Mist both sides of each tender with cooking spray.
4. To prep the Utica greens: In the Zone 2 basket, mix the greens, prosciutto, cherry peppers, garlic powder, onion powder, and salt. Scatter the bread crumbs and Romano cheese over the top. Spritz the greens with cooking spray.
5. To cook the chicken and greens:
6. Install a crisper plate in the Zone 1 basket. Place the chicken tenders in the basket in a single layer and insert the basket in the unit. Insert the Zone 2 basket in the unit.
7. Select Zone 1, select AIR FRY, set the temperature to 390°F, and set the time to 25 minutes.
8. Select Zone 2, select AIR BROIL, set the temperature to 450°F, and set the time to 10 minutes. Select SMART FINISH.
9. Press START/PAUSE to begin cooking.
10. When cooking is complete, the chicken will be crispy and cooked through and the greens should be warmed through and toasted on top. Serve warm.

Asian Chicken

Servings: 4
Cooking Time: 12 Minutes
Ingredients:
- 8 chicken thighs, boneless
- 4 garlic cloves, minced
- 85g honey
- 120ml soy sauce
- 1 tsp dried oregano
- 2 tbsp parsley, chopped
- 1 tbsp ketchup

Directions:
1. Add chicken and remaining ingredients in a bowl and mix until well coated. Cover and place in the refrigerator for 6 hours.
2. Insert a crisper plate in the Tefal air fryer baskets.
3. Remove the chicken from the marinade and place them in both baskets.
4. Select zone 1 then select "air fry" mode and set the temperature to 390 degrees F for 12 minutes. Press "match" to match zone 2 settings to zone 1. Press "start/stop" to begin.

Nutrition:
- (Per serving) Calories 646 | Fat 21.7g |Sodium 2092mg | Carbs 22.2g | Fiber 0.6g | Sugar 18.9g | Protein 86.9g

Greek Chicken Souvlaki

Servings: 3 To 4
Cooking Time: 15 Minutes

Ingredients:

- Chicken:
- Grated zest and juice of 1 lemon
- 2 tablespoons extra-virgin olive oil
- 1 tablespoon Greek souvlaki seasoning
- 450 g boneless, skinless chicken breast, cut into 2-inch chunks
- Vegetable oil spray
- For Serving:
- Warm pita bread or hot cooked rice
- Sliced ripe tomatoes
- Sliced cucumbers
- Thinly sliced red onion
- Kalamata olives
- Tzatziki

Directions:

1. For the chicken: In a small bowl, combine the lemon zest, lemon juice, olive oil, and souvlaki seasoning. Place the chicken in a gallon-size resealable plastic bag. Pour the marinade over chicken. Seal bag and massage to coat. Place the bag in a large bowl and marinate for 30 minutes, or cover and refrigerate up to 24 hours, turning the bag occasionally. 2. Place the chicken a single layer in the zone 1 air fryer drawer. Cook at 180ºC for 10 minutes, turning the chicken and spraying with a little vegetable oil spray halfway through the cooking time. Increase the air fryer temperature to 200ºC for 5 minutes to allow the chicken to crisp and brown a little. 3. Transfer the chicken to a serving platter and serve with pita bread or rice, tomatoes, cucumbers, onion, olives and tzatziki.

Juicy Paprika Chicken Breast

Servings: 4
Cooking Time: 30 Minutes

Ingredients:

- Oil, for spraying
- 4 (170 g) boneless, skinless chicken breasts
- 1 tablespoon olive oil
- 1 tablespoon paprika
- 1 tablespoon packed light brown sugar
- ½ teaspoon cayenne pepper
- ½ teaspoon onion powder
- ½ teaspoon granulated garlic

Directions:

1. Line the two air fryer drawers with parchment and spray lightly with oil.
2. Brush the chicken with the olive oil.
3. In a small bowl, mix together the paprika, brown sugar, cayenne pepper, onion powder, and garlic and sprinkle it over the chicken.
4. Place the chicken in the two prepared drawers.
5. Air fry at 180ºC for 15 minutes, flip, and cook for another 15 minutes, or until the internal temperature reaches 76ºC. Serve immediately.

Cajun Chicken With Vegetables

Servings: 6
Cooking Time: 20 Minutes

Ingredients:

- 450g chicken breast, boneless & diced
- 1 tbsp Cajun seasoning
- 400g grape tomatoes
- ⅛ tsp dried thyme
- ⅛ tsp dried oregano
- 1 tsp smoked paprika
- 1 zucchini, diced
- 30ml olive oil
- 1 bell pepper, diced
- 1 tsp onion powder
- 1 ½ tsp garlic powder
- Pepper
- Salt

Directions:

1. In a bowl, toss chicken with vegetables, oil, herb, spices, and salt until well coated.
2. Insert a crisper plate in the Tefal air fryer baskets.
3. Add chicken and vegetable mixture to both baskets.
4. Select zone 1, then select "air fry" mode and set the temperature to 390 degrees F for 20 minutes. Press "match" to match zone 2 settings to zone 1. Press "start/stop" to begin.

Nutrition:

- (Per serving) Calories 153 | Fat 6.9g |Sodium 98mg | Carbs 6g | Fiber 1.6g | Sugar 3.5g | Protein 17.4g

Chicken Thighs With Coriander

Servings: 4
Cooking Time: 25 Minutes
Ingredients:
- 1 tablespoon olive oil
- Juice of ½ lime
- 1 tablespoon coconut aminos
- 1½ teaspoons Montreal chicken seasoning
- 8 bone-in chicken thighs, skin on
- 2 tablespoons chopped fresh coriander

Directions:
1. In a gallon-size resealable bag, combine the olive oil, lime juice, coconut aminos, and chicken seasoning. Add the chicken thighs, seal the bag, and massage the bag to ensure the chicken is thoroughly coated. Refrigerate for at least 2 hours, preferably overnight.
2. Preheat the air fryer to 200°C.
3. Remove the chicken from the marinade and arrange in a single layer in the two air fryer baskets. Pausing halfway through the cooking time to flip the chicken, air fry for 20 to 25 minutes, until a thermometer inserted into the thickest part registers 75°C.
4. Transfer the chicken to a serving platter and top with the coriander before serving.

Spicy Chicken Sandwiches With "fried" Pickles

Servings: 4
Cooking Time: 18 Minutes
Ingredients:
- FOR THE CHICKEN SANDWICHES
- 2 tablespoons all-purpose flour
- 2 large eggs
- 2 teaspoons Louisiana-style hot sauce
- 1 cup panko bread crumbs
- 1 teaspoon paprika
- ½ teaspoon garlic powder
- ¼ teaspoon salt
- ¼ teaspoon freshly ground black pepper
- ¼ teaspoon cayenne pepper (optional)
- 4 thin-sliced chicken cutlets (4 ounces each)
- 2 teaspoons vegetable oil
- 4 hamburger rolls
- FOR THE PICKLES
- 1 cup dill pickle chips, drained
- 1 large egg
- ½ cup panko bread crumbs
- Nonstick cooking spray
- ½ cup ranch dressing, for serving (optional)

Directions:
1. To prep the sandwiches:
2. Set up a breading station with three small shallow bowls. Place the flour in the first bowl. In the second bowl, whisk together the eggs and hot sauce. Combine the panko, paprika, garlic powder, salt, black pepper, and cayenne pepper in the third bowl.
3. Bread the chicken cutlets in this order: First, dip them into the flour, coating both sides. Then, dip into the egg mixture. Finally, coat them in the panko mixture, gently pressing the breading into the chicken to help it adhere. Drizzle the cutlets with the oil.
4. To prep the pickles:
5. Pat the pickles dry with a paper towel.
6. In a small shallow bowl, whisk the egg. Add the panko to a second shallow bowl.
7. Dip the pickles in the egg, then the panko. Mist both sides of the pickles with cooking spray.
8. To cook the chicken and pickles:
9. Install a crisper plate in each of the two baskets. Place the chicken in the Zone 1 basket and insert the basket in the unit. Place the pickles in the Zone 2 basket and insert the basket in the unit.
10. Select Zone 1, select AIR FRY, set the temperature to 390°F, and set the time to 18 minutes.
11. Select Zone 2, select AIR FRY, set the temperature to 400°F, and set the time to 15 minutes. Select SMART FINISH.
12. Press START/PAUSE to begin cooking.
13. When both timers read 10 minutes, press START/PAUSE. Remove the Zone 1 basket and use silicone-tipped tongs to flip the chicken. Reinsert the basket. Remove the Zone 2 basket and shake to redistribute the pickles. Reinsert the basket and press START/PAUSE to resume cooking.
14. When cooking is complete, the breading will be crisp and golden brown and the chicken cooked through . Place one chicken cutlet on each hamburger roll. Serve the "fried" pickles on the side with ranch dressing, if desired.

Maple-mustard Glazed Turkey Tenderloin With Apple And Sage Stuffing

Servings: 4
Cooking Time: 35 Minutes
Ingredients:
- FOR THE TURKEY TENDERLOIN
- 2 tablespoons maple syrup
- 1 tablespoon unsalted butter, at room temperature
- 1 tablespoon Dijon mustard
- ½ teaspoon kosher salt
- ½ teaspoon freshly ground black pepper
- 1½ pounds turkey tenderloin
- FOR THE STUFFING
- 6 ounces seasoned stuffing mix
- 1½ cups chicken broth
- 1 apple, peeled, cored, and diced
- 1 tablespoon chopped fresh sage
- 2 teaspoons unsalted butter, cut into several pieces

Directions:
1. To prep the turkey tenderloin: In a small bowl, mix the maple syrup, butter, mustard, salt, and black pepper until smooth. Spread the maple mixture over the entire turkey tenderloin.
2. To prep the stuffing: In the Zone 2 basket, combine the stuffing mix and chicken broth. Stir well to ensure the bread is fully moistened. Stir in the apple and sage. Scatter the butter on top.
3. To cook the turkey and stuffing:
4. Install a crisper plate in the Zone 1 basket. Place the turkey tenderloin in the basket and insert the basket in the unit. Insert the Zone 2 basket in the unit.
5. Select Zone 1, select AIR FRY, set the temperature to 390°F, and set the time to 35 minutes.
6. Select Zone 2, select BAKE, set the temperature to 340°F, and set the time to 20 minutes. Select SMART FINISH.
7. Press START/PAUSE to begin cooking.
8. When the Zone 2 timer reads 10 minutes, press START/PAUSE. Remove the basket and stir the stuffing. Reinsert the basket and press START/PAUSE to resume cooking.
9. When cooking is complete, the turkey will be cooked through and the stuffing will have absorbed all the liquid and be slightly crisp on top. Serve warm.

Bruschetta Chicken

Servings: 4
Cooking Time: 20 Minutes
Ingredients:
- Bruschetta Stuffing:
- 1 tomato, diced
- 3 tablespoons balsamic vinegar
- 1 teaspoon Italian seasoning
- 2 tablespoons chopped fresh basil
- 3 garlic cloves, minced
- 2 tablespoons extra-virgin olive oil
- Chicken:
- 4 (115 g) boneless, skinless chicken breasts, cut 4 slits each
- 1 teaspoon Italian seasoning
- Chicken seasoning or rub, to taste
- Cooking spray

Directions:
1. Preheat the air fryer to 190°. Spritz the two air fryer baskets with cooking spray.
2. Combine the ingredients for the bruschetta stuffing in a bowl. Stir to mix well. Set aside.
3. Rub the chicken breasts with Italian seasoning and chicken seasoning on a clean work surface.
4. Arrange the chicken breasts, slits side up, in a single layer in the two air fryer baskets and spritz with cooking spray.
5. Air fry for 7 minutes, then open the air fryer and fill the slits in the chicken with the bruschetta stuffing. Cook for another 3 minutes or until the chicken is well browned.
6. Serve immediately.

Italian Chicken & Potatoes

Servings: 4
Cooking Time: 24 Minutes
Ingredients:

- 450g chicken breast, boneless & diced
- 30ml olive oil
- ½ tsp lemon zest
- 2 tbsp fresh lemon juice
- 450g baby potatoes, quartered
- 1 tbsp Greek seasoning
- Pepper
- Salt

Directions:

1. Toss potatoes with ½ tablespoon Greek seasoning, 1 tablespoon oil, lemon zest, lemon juice, pepper, and salt in a bowl.
2. Insert a crisper plate in the Tefal air fryer baskets.
3. Add potatoes into the zone 1 basket.
4. In a bowl, toss chicken with the remaining oil and seasoning.
5. Add the chicken into the zone 2 basket.
6. Select zone 1, then select "air fry" mode and set the temperature to 390 degrees F for 12 minutes. Press "match" to match zone 2 settings to zone 1. Press "start/stop" to begin.

Nutrition:

- (Per serving) Calories 262 | Fat 10.1g |Sodium 227mg | Carbs 15.5g | Fiber 2.9g | Sugar 0.2g | Protein 27.2g

Orange Chicken With Roasted Snap Peas And Scallions

Servings: 4
Cooking Time: 30 Minutes
Ingredients:

- FOR THE CHICKEN
- ⅓ cup all-purpose flour
- 2 large eggs
- ⅓ cup cornstarch, plus 2 tablespoons
- 1½ pounds boneless, skinless chicken breasts, cut into 1-inch pieces
- Nonstick cooking spray
- 2 tablespoons grated orange zest
- 1 cup freshly squeezed orange juice
- ¼ cup granulated sugar
- 2 tablespoons rice vinegar
- 2 tablespoons soy sauce
- ¼ teaspoon minced fresh ginger
- ¼ teaspoon grated garlic
- FOR THE SNAP PEAS
- 8 ounces snap peas
- 1 tablespoon vegetable oil
- ½ teaspoon minced garlic
- ½ teaspoon grated fresh ginger
- ¼ teaspoon kosher salt
- ¼ teaspoon freshly ground black pepper
- 4 scallions, thinly sliced

Directions:

1. To prep the chicken:
2. Set up a breading station with three small shallow bowls. Place the flour in the first bowl. In the second bowl, beat the eggs. Place ⅓ cup of cornstarch in the third bowl.
3. Bread the chicken pieces in this order: First, dip them into the flour to coat. Then, dip into the beaten egg. Finally, add them to the cornstarch, coating all sides. Mist the breaded chicken with cooking spray.
4. In a small bowl, whisk together the orange zest, orange juice, sugar, vinegar, soy sauce, ginger, garlic, and remaining 2 tablespoons of cornstarch. Set orange sauce aside.
5. To prep the snap peas: In a large bowl, combine the snap peas, oil, garlic, ginger, salt, and black pepper. Toss to coat.
6. To cook the chicken and snap peas: Install a crisper plate in the Zone 1 basket. Add the chicken to the basket and insert the basket in the unit. Place the snap peas in the Zone 2 basket and insert the basket in the unit.
7. Select Zone 1, select AIR FRY, set the temperature to 400°F, and set the time to 30 minutes.
8. Select Zone 2, select ROAST, set the temperature to 375°F, and set the time to 12 minutes. Select SMART FINISH.
9. Press START/PAUSE to begin cooking.
10. When the Zone 1 timer reads 15 minutes, press START/PAUSE. Remove the basket and shake to redistribute the chicken. Reinsert the basket and press START/PAUSE to resume cooking.
11. When the Zone 1 timer reads 5 minutes, press START/PAUSE. Remove the basket and pour the reserved orange sauce over the chicken. Reinsert the basket and press START/PAUSE to resume cooking.
12. When cooking is complete, the chicken and vegetables will be cooked through. Stir the scallions into the snap peas. Serve hot.

Nashville Hot Chicken

Servings: 8
Cooking Time: 24 To 28 Minutes
Ingredients:

- 1.4 kg bone-in, skin-on chicken pieces, breasts halved crosswise
- 1 tablespoon sea salt
- 1 tablespoon freshly ground black pepper
- 140 g finely ground blanched almond flour
- 130 g grated Parmesan cheese
- 1 tablespoon baking powder
- 2 teaspoons garlic powder, divided
- 120 g heavy (whipping) cream
- 2 large eggs, beaten
- 1 tablespoon vinegar-based hot sauce
- Avocado oil spray
- 115 g unsalted butter
- 120 ml avocado oil
- 1 tablespoon cayenne pepper (more or less to taste)
- 2 tablespoons Xylitol

Directions:

1. Sprinkle the chicken with the salt and pepper.
2. In a large shallow bowl, whisk together the almond flour, Parmesan cheese, baking powder, and 1 teaspoon of the garlic powder.
3. In a separate bowl, whisk together the heavy cream, eggs, and hot sauce.
4. Dip the chicken pieces in the egg, then coat each with the almond flour mixture, pressing the mixture into the chicken to adhere. Allow to sit for 15 minutes to let the breading set.
5. Set the air fryer to 200°C. Place the chicken in a single layer in the two air fryer baskets, being careful not to overcrowd the pieces. Spray the chicken with oil and roast for 13 minutes.
6. Carefully flip the chicken and spray it with more oil. Reduce the air fryer temperature to 180°C. Roast for another 11 to 15 minutes, until an instant-read thermometer reads 70°C.
7. While the chicken cooks, heat the butter, avocado oil, cayenne pepper, xylitol, and remaining 1 teaspoon of garlic powder in a saucepan over medium-low heat. Cook until the butter is melted and the sugar substitute has dissolved.
8. Remove the chicken from the air fryer. Use tongs to dip the chicken in the sauce. Place the coated chicken on a rack over a baking sheet, and allow it to rest for 5 minutes before serving.

Crispy Dill Chicken Strips

Servings: 4
Cooking Time: 10 Minutes
Ingredients:

- 2 whole boneless, skinless chicken breasts (about 450 g each), halved lengthwise
- 230 ml Italian dressing
- 110 g finely crushed crisps
- 1 tablespoon dried dill weed
- 1 tablespoon garlic powder
- 1 large egg, beaten
- 1 to 2 tablespoons oil

Directions:

1. In a large resealable bag, combine the chicken and Italian dressing. Seal the bag and refrigerate to marinate at least 1 hour.
2. In a shallow dish, stir together the potato chips, dill, and garlic powder. Place the beaten egg in a second shallow dish.
3. Remove the chicken from the marinade. Roll the chicken pieces in the egg and the crisp mixture, coating thoroughly.
4. Preheat the air fryer to 170°C. Line the two air fryer drawers with parchment paper.
5. Place the coated chicken on the parchment and spritz with oil.
6. Cook for 5 minutes. Flip the chicken, spritz it with oil, and cook for 5 minutes more until the outsides are crispy and the insides are no longer pink.

Chipotle Drumsticks

Servings: 4
Cooking Time: 20 Minutes
Ingredients:

- 1 tablespoon tomato paste
- ½ teaspoon chipotle powder
- ¼ teaspoon apple cider vinegar
- ¼ teaspoon garlic powder
- 8 chicken drumsticks
- ½ teaspoon salt
- ⅛ teaspoon ground black pepper

Directions:

1. In a small bowl, combine tomato paste, chipotle powder, vinegar, and garlic powder.
2. Sprinkle drumsticks with salt and pepper, then place into a large bowl and pour in tomato paste mixture. Toss or stir to evenly coat all drumsticks in mixture.
3. Place drumsticks into two ungreased air fryer baskets. Adjust the temperature to 200°C and air fry for 25 minutes, turning drumsticks halfway through cooking. Drumsticks will be dark red with an internal temperature of at least 75°C when done. Serve warm.

Turkey Burger Patties

Servings: 4
Cooking Time: 14 Minutes
Ingredients:

- 1 egg white
- 453g ground turkey
- 30ml Worcestershire sauce
- ½ tsp dried basil
- ½ tsp dried oregano
- Pepper
- Salt

Directions:

1. In a bowl, mix ground turkey with remaining ingredients until well combined.
2. Insert a crisper plate in the Tefal air fryer baskets.
3. Make patties from the turkey mixture and place them in both baskets.
4. Select zone 1, then select "air fry" mode and set the temperature to 360 degrees F for 14 minutes. Press "match" to match zone 2 settings to zone 1. Press "start/stop" to begin.

Nutrition:

- (Per serving) Calories 234 | Fat 12.5g |Sodium 251mg | Carbs 1.7g | Fiber 0.1g | Sugar 1.6g | Protein 32g

Bacon-wrapped Chicken

Servings: 2
Cooking Time: 28 Minutes
Ingredients:

- Butter:
- ½ stick butter softened
- ½ garlic clove, minced
- ¼ teaspoon dried thyme
- ¼ teaspoon dried basil
- ⅛ teaspoon coarse salt
- 1 pinch black pepper, ground
- ⅓ lb. thick-cut bacon
- 1 ½ lbs. boneless skinless chicken thighs
- 2 teaspoons garlic, minced

Directions:

1. Mix garlic softened butter with thyme, salt, basil, and black pepper in a bowl.
2. Add butter mixture on a piece of wax paper and roll it up tightly to make a butter log.
3. Place the log in the refrigerator for 2 hours.
4. Spray one bacon strip on a piece of wax paper.
5. Place each chicken thigh on top of one bacon strip and rub it with garlic.

6. Make a slit in the chicken thigh and add a teaspoon of butter to the chicken.
7. Wrap the bacon around the chicken thigh.
8. Repeat those same steps with all the chicken thighs.
9. Place the bacon-wrapped chicken thighs in the two crisper plates.
10. Return the crisper plates to the Tefal Dual Zone Air Fryer.
11. Choose the Air Fry mode for Zone 1 and set the temperature to 390 degrees F and the time to 28 minutes|
12. Select the "MATCH" button to copy the settings for Zone 2.
13. Initiate cooking by pressing the START/STOP button.
14. Flip the chicken once cooked halfway through, and resume cooking.
15. Serve warm.

Turkey And Cranberry Quesadillas

Servings: 4
Cooking Time: 4 To 8 Minutes
Ingredients:

- 6 low-sodium whole-wheat tortillas
- 75 g shredded low-sodium low-fat Swiss cheese
- 105 g shredded cooked low-sodium turkey breast
- 2 tablespoons cranberry sauce
- 2 tablespoons dried cranberries
- ½ teaspoon dried basil
- Olive oil spray, for spraying the tortillas

Directions:

1. Preheat the air fryer to 200°C.
2. Put 3 tortillas on a work surface.
3. Evenly divide the Swiss cheese, turkey, cranberry sauce, and dried cranberries among the tortillas. Sprinkle with the basil and top with the remaining tortillas.
4. Spray the outsides of the tortillas with olive oil spray.
5. One at a time, air fry the quesadillas in the air fryer for 4 to 8 minutes, or until crisp and the cheese is melted. Cut into quarters and serve.

Brazilian Chicken Drumsticks

Servings: 6
Cooking Time: 47 Minutes
Ingredients:

- 2 teaspoons cumin seeds
- 2 teaspoons dried parsley
- 2 teaspoons turmeric powder
- 2 teaspoons dried oregano leaves
- 2 teaspoons salt
- 1 teaspoon coriander seeds
- 1 teaspoon black peppercorns
- 1 teaspoon cayenne pepper
- ½ cup lime juice
- 4 tablespoons vegetable oil
- 3 lbs. chicken drumsticks

Directions:

1. Grind cumin, parsley, salt, coriander seeds, cayenne pepper, peppercorns, oregano, and turmeric in a food processor.
2. Add this mixture to lemon juice and oil in a bowl and mix well.
3. Rub the spice paste over the chicken drumsticks and let them marinate for 30 minutes|
4. Divide the chicken drumsticks in both the crisper plates.
5. Return the crisper plates to the Tefal Dual Zone Air Fryer.
6. Choose the Air Fry mode for Zone 1 and set the temperature to 390 degrees F and the time to 47 minutes|
7. Select the "MATCH" button to copy the settings for Zone 2.
8. Initiate cooking by pressing the START/STOP button.
9. Flip the drumsticks when cooked halfway through, then resume cooking.
10. Serve warm.

Stuffed Chicken Florentine

Servings: 4
Cooking Time: 20 Minutes
Ingredients:

- 3 tablespoons pine nuts
- 40 g frozen spinach, thawed and squeezed dry
- 75 g ricotta cheese
- 2 tablespoons grated Parmesan cheese
- 3 cloves garlic, minced
- Salt and freshly ground black pepper, to taste
- 4 small boneless, skinless chicken breast halves (about 680 g)
- 8 slices bacon

Directions:

1. In a large bowl, combine the spinach, ricotta, Parmesan, and garlic. Season to taste with salt and pepper and stir well until thoroughly combined.
2. Using a sharp knife, cut into the chicken breasts, slicing them across and opening them up like a book, but be careful not to cut them all the way through. Sprinkle the chicken with salt and pepper.
3. Spoon equal amounts of the spinach mixture into the chicken, then fold the top of the chicken breast back over the top of the stuffing. Wrap each chicken breast with 2 slices of bacon.
4. Air fry the chicken for 18 to 20 minutes in zone 1 drawer until the bacon is crisp and a thermometer inserted into the thickest part of the chicken registers 76°C.
5. Place the pine nuts in a small pan and set in the zone 2 air fryer drawer. Air fry at 200°C for 2 to 3 minutes until toasted. Remove the pine nuts to a mixing bowl.

Coriander Lime Chicken Thighs

Servings: 4
Cooking Time: 22 Minutes
Ingredients:

- 4 bone-in, skin-on chicken thighs
- 1 teaspoon baking powder
- ½ teaspoon garlic powder
- 2 teaspoons chili powder
- 1 teaspoon cumin
- 2 medium limes
- 5 g chopped fresh coriander

Directions:

1. Pat chicken thighs dry and sprinkle with baking powder.
2. In a small bowl, mix garlic powder, chili powder, and cumin and sprinkle evenly over thighs, gently rubbing on and under chicken skin.
3. Cut one lime in half and squeeze juice over thighs. Place chicken into the zone 1 air fryer drawer.
4. Adjust the temperature to 190°C and roast for 22 minutes.
5. Cut other lime into four wedges for serving and garnish cooked chicken with wedges and coriander.

Teriyaki Chicken Skewers

Servings: 4
Cooking Time: 16 Minutes

Ingredients:
- 455g boneless chicken thighs, cubed
- 237ml teriyaki marinade
- 16 small wooden skewers
- Sesame seeds for rolling
- Teriyaki Marinade
- ⅓ cup soy sauce
- 59ml chicken broth
- ½ orange, juiced
- 2 tablespoons brown sugar
- 1 teaspoon ginger, grated
- 1 clove garlic, grated

Directions:
1. Blend teriyaki marinade ingredients in a blender.
2. Add chicken and its marinade to a Ziplock bag.
3. Seal this bag, shake it well and refrigerate for 30 minutes.
4. Thread the chicken on the wooden skewers.
5. Place these skewers in the air fryer baskets.
6. Return the air fryer basket 1 to Zone 1, and basket 2 to Zone 2 of the Tefal 2-Basket Air Fryer.
7. Choose the "Air Fry" mode for Zone 1 at 350 degrees F and 16 minutes of cooking time.
8. Select the "MATCH COOK" option to copy the settings for Zone 2.
9. Initiate cooking by pressing the START/PAUSE BUTTON.
10. Flip the skewers once cooked halfway through.
11. Garnish with sesame seeds.
12. Serve warm.

Nutrition:
- (Per serving) Calories 456 | Fat 16.4g |Sodium 1321mg | Carbs 19.2g | Fiber 2.2g | Sugar 4.2g | Protein 55.2g

Chicken Thighs In Waffles

Servings: 4
Cooking Time: 40 Minutes

Ingredients:
- For the chicken:
- 4 chicken thighs, skin on
- 240 ml low-fat buttermilk
- 65 g all-purpose flour
- ½ teaspoon garlic powder
- ½ teaspoon mustard powder
- 1 teaspoon kosher salt
- ½ teaspoon freshly ground black pepper
- 85 g honey, for serving
- Cooking spray
- For the waffles:
- 65 g all-purpose flour
- 65 g whole wheat pastry flour
- 1 large egg, beaten
- 240 ml low-fat buttermilk
- 1 teaspoon baking powder
- 2 tablespoons rapeseed oil
- ½ teaspoon kosher salt
- 1 tablespoon granulated sugar

Directions:
1. Combine the chicken thighs with buttermilk in a large bowl. Wrap the bowl in plastic and refrigerate to marinate for at least an hour. 2. Preheat the air fryer to 180°C. Spritz the two air fryer baskets with cooking spray. 3. Combine the flour, mustard powder, garlic powder, salt, and black pepper in a shallow dish. Stir to mix well. 4. Remove the thighs from the buttermilk and pat dry with paper towels. Sit the bowl of buttermilk aside. 5. Dip the thighs in the flour mixture first, then into the buttermilk, and then into the flour mixture. Shake the excess off. 6. Arrange the thighs in the two preheated air fryer baskets and spritz with cooking spray. Air fryer for 20 minutes or until an instant-read thermometer inserted in the thickest part of the chicken thighs registers at least 75°C. Flip the thighs halfway through. 7. Meanwhile, make the waffles: combine the ingredients for the waffles in a large bowl. Stir to mix well, then arrange the mixture in a waffle iron and cook until a golden and fragrant waffle forms. 8. Remove the waffles from the waffle iron and slice into 4 pieces. Remove the chicken thighs from the air fryer and allow to cool for 5 minutes. 9. Arrange each chicken thigh on each waffle piece and drizzle with 1 tablespoon of honey. Serve warm.

Juicy Duck Breast

Servings: 1
Cooking Time: 20 Minutes

Ingredients:

- ½ duck breast
- Salt and black pepper, to taste
- 2 tablespoons plum sauce

Directions:

1. Rub the duck breast with black pepper and salt.
2. Place the duck breast in air fryer basket 1 and add plum sauce on top.
3. Return the basket to the Tefal 2 Baskets Air Fryer.
4. Choose the "Air Fry" mode for Zone 1 and set the temperature to 400 degrees F and 20 minutes of cooking time.
5. Initiate cooking by pressing the START/PAUSE BUTTON.
6. Flip the duck breast once cooked halfway through.
7. Serve warm.

Nutrition:

- (Per serving) Calories 379 | Fat 19g |Sodium 184mg | Carbs 12.3g | Fiber 0.6g | Sugar 2g | Protein 37.7g

Crispy Sesame Chicken

Servings: 2
Cooking Time: 10 Minutes

Ingredients:

- 680g boneless chicken thighs, diced
- 2 tablespoons rice vinegar
- 1 tablespoon soy sauce
- 2 teaspoons minced fresh ginger
- 1 garlic clove, minced
- ¾ teaspoon salt
- ½ teaspoon black pepper
- 2 large eggs, beaten
- 1 cup cornstarch
- Sauce
- 59ml soy sauce
- 2 tablespoons rice vinegar
- ⅓ cup brown sugar
- 59ml water
- 1 tablespoon cornstarch
- 2 teaspoons sesame oil
- 2 tablespoons vegetable oil
- 2 garlic cloves, minced
- 2 teaspoons chile paste
- Garnish
- 1 tablespoon toasted sesame seeds

Directions:

1. Blend all the sauce ingredients in a saucepan and cook until it thickens then allow it to cool.
2. Mix chicken with black pepper, salt, garlic, ginger, vinegar, and soy sauce in a bowl.
3. Cover and marinate the chicken for 20 minutes.
4. Divide the chicken in the air fryer baskets.
5. Return the air fryer basket 1 to Zone 1, and basket 2 to Zone 2 of the Tefal 2-Basket Air Fryer.
6. Choose the "Air Fry" mode for Zone 1 and set the temperature to 400 degrees F and 10 minutes of cooking time.
7. Select the "MATCH COOK" option to copy the settings for Zone 2.
8. Initiate cooking by pressing the START/PAUSE BUTTON.
9. Pour the prepared sauce over the air fried chicken and drizzle sesame seeds on top.
10. Serve warm.

Nutrition:

- (Per serving) Calories 351 | Fat 16g |Sodium 777mg | Carbs 26g | Fiber 4g | Sugar 5g | Protein 28g

Fish And Seafood Recipes

Fish Fillets With Lemon-dill Sauce

Servings: 4
Cooking Time: 7 Minutes
Ingredients:

- 455 g snapper, grouper, or salmon fillets
- Sea salt and freshly ground black pepper, to taste
- 1 tablespoon avocado oil
- 60 g sour cream
- 60 g mayonnaise
- 2 tablespoons fresh dill, chopped, plus more for garnish
- 1 tablespoon freshly squeezed lemon juice
- ½ teaspoon grated lemon zest

Directions:
1. Pat the fish dry with paper towels and season well with salt and pepper. Brush with the avocado oil. 2. Set the air fryer to 204°C. Place the fillets in the two air fryer drawers and air fry for 1 minute. 3. Lower the air fryer temperature to 164°C and continue cooking for 5 minutes. Flip the fish and cook for 1 minute more or until an instant-read thermometer reads 64°C. 4. While the fish is cooking, make the sauce by combining the sour cream, mayonnaise, dill, lemon juice, and lemon zest in a medium bowl. Season with salt and pepper and stir until combined. Refrigerate until ready to serve. 5. Serve the fish with the sauce, garnished with the remaining dill.

Prawn Creole Casserole And Garlic Lemon Scallops

Servings: 8
Cooking Time: 25 Minutes
Ingredients:

- Prawn Creole Casserole:
- 360 g prawns, peeled and deveined
- 50 g chopped celery
- 50 g chopped onion
- 50 g chopped green bell pepper
- 2 large eggs, beaten
- 240 ml single cream
- 1 tablespoon butter, melted
- 1 tablespoon cornflour
- 1 teaspoon Creole seasoning
- ¾ teaspoon salt
- ½ teaspoon freshly ground black pepper
- 120 g shredded Cheddar cheese
- Cooking spray
- Garlic Lemon Scallops:
- 4 tablespoons salted butter, melted
- 4 teaspoons peeled and finely minced garlic
- ½ small lemon, zested and juiced
- 8 sea scallops, 30 g each, cleaned and patted dry
- ¼ teaspoon salt
- ¼ teaspoon ground black pepper

Directions:
1. Make the Prawn Creole Casserole :
2. In a medium bowl, stir together the prawns, celery, onion, and green pepper.
3. In another medium bowl, whisk the eggs, single cream, butter, cornflour, Creole seasoning, salt, and pepper until blended. Stir the egg mixture into the prawn mixture. Add the cheese and stir to combine.
4. Preheat the air fryer to 150°C. Spritz a baking pan with oil.
5. Transfer the prawn mixture to the prepared pan and place it in the zone 1 air fryer drawer.
6. Bake for 25 minutes, stirring every 10 minutes, until a knife inserted into the center comes out clean.
7. Serve immediately.
8. Make the Garlic Lemon Scallops :
9. In a small bowl, mix butter, garlic, lemon zest, and lemon juice. Place scallops in an ungreased round nonstick baking dish. Pour butter mixture over scallops, then sprinkle with salt and pepper.
10. Place dish into the zone 2 air fryer drawer. Adjust the temperature to 182°C and bake for 10 minutes. Scallops will be opaque and firm, and have an internal temperature of 56°C when done. Serve warm.

Seafood Shrimp Omelet

Servings:2
Cooking Time:15
Ingredients:
- 6 large shrimp, shells removed and chopped
- 6 eggs, beaten
- ½ tablespoon of butter, melted
- 2 tablespoons green onions, sliced
- 1/3 cup of mushrooms, chopped
- 1 pinch paprika
- Salt and black pepper, to taste
- Oil spray, for greasing

Directions:
1. In a large bowl whisk the eggs and add chopped shrimp, butter, green onions, mushrooms, paprika, salt, and black pepper.
2. Take two cake pans that fit inside the air fryer and grease them with oil spray.
3. Pour the egg mixture between the cake pans and place it in two baskets of the air fryer.
4. Turn on the BAKE function of zone 1, and let it cook for 15 minutes at 320 degrees F.
5. Select the MATCH button to match the cooking time for the zone 2 basket.
6. Once the cooking cycle completes, take out, and serve hot.

Nutrition:
- (Per serving) Calories 300 | Fat 17.5g| Sodium 368mg | Carbs 2.9g | Fiber 0.3g | Sugar1.4 g | Protein32.2 g

Beer Battered Fish Fillet

Servings:2
Cooking Time:14
Ingredients:
- 1 cup all-purpose flour
- 4 tablespoons cornstarch
- 1 teaspoon baking soda
- 8 ounces beer
- 2 egg beaten
- ½ cup all-purpose flour
- 1 teaspoon smoked paprika
- 1 teaspoon salt
- 1/4 teaspoon freshly ground black pepper
- ¼ teaspoon of cayenne pepper
- 2 cod fillets, 1½-inches thick, cut into 4 pieces
- Oil spray, for greasing

Directions:

1. Take a large bowl and combine flour, baking soda, corn starch, and salt
2. In a separate bowl beat eggs along with the beer.
3. In a shallow dish mix paprika, salt, pepper, and cayenne pepper.
4. Dry the codfish fillets with a paper towel.
5. Dip the fish into the eggs and coat it with seasoned flour.
6. Then dip it in the seasoning.
7. Grease the fillet with oil spray.
8. Divide the fillet between both zones.
9. Set zone 1 to AIR FRY mode at 400 degrees F for 14 minutes.
10. Select MACTH button for zone 2 basket.
11. Press start and let the AIR fry do its magic.
12. Once cooking is done, serve the fish.
13. Enjoy it hot.

Nutrition:
- (Per serving) Calories 1691| Fat 6.1g| Sodium 3976mg | Carbs105.1 g | Fiber 3.4g | Sugar15.6 g | Protein 270g

Perfect Parmesan Salmon

Servings: 4
Cooking Time:10 Minutes
Ingredients:
- 4 salmon fillets
- 1/4 cup parmesan cheese, shredded
- 1/4 tsp dried dill
- 1/2 tbsp Dijon mustard
- 4 tbsp mayonnaise
- 1 lemon juice
- Pepper
- Salt

Directions:
1. In a small bowl, mix cheese, dill, mustard, mayonnaise, lemon juice, pepper, and salt.
2. Place salmon fillets into the air fryer basket and brush with cheese mixture.
3. Cook salmon fillets at 400 F for 10 minutes.
4. Serve and enjoy.

Tilapia With Mojo And Crispy Plantains

Servings:4
Cooking Time: 30 Minutes
Ingredients:
- FOR THE TILAPIA
- 4 tilapia fillets (6 ounces each)
- 2 tablespoons all-purpose flour
- Nonstick cooking spray
- ¼ cup freshly squeezed orange juice
- 3 tablespoons fresh lime juice
- 2 tablespoons olive oil
- 1 tablespoon minced garlic
- ½ teaspoon ground cumin
- ¼ teaspoon kosher salt
- FOR THE PLANTAINS
- 1 large green plantain
- 2 cups cold water
- 2 teaspoons kosher salt
- Nonstick cooking spray

Directions:
1. To prep the tilapia: Dust both sides of the tilapia fillets with the flour, then spritz with cooking spray.
2. In a small bowl, whisk together the orange juice, lime juice, oil, garlic, cumin, and salt. Set the mojo sauce aside.
3. To prep the plantains: Cut the ends from the plantain, then remove and discard the peel. Slice the plantain into 1-inch rounds.
4. In a large bowl, combine the water, salt, and plantains. Let soak for 15 minutes.
5. Drain the plantains and pat them dry with paper towels. Spray with cooking spray.
6. To cook the tilapia and plantains: Install a crisper plate in each of the two baskets. Place the tilapia in a single layer in the Zone 1 basket (work in batches if needed) and insert the basket in the unit. Place the plantains in the Zone 2 basket and insert the basket in the unit.
7. Select Zone 1, select AIR FRY, set the temperature to 390°F, and set the timer to 10 minutes.
8. Select Zone 2, select AIR FRY, set the temperature to 390°F, and set the timer to 30 minutes. Select SMART FINISH.
9. Press START/PAUSE to begin cooking.
10. When the Zone 2 timer reads 10 minutes, press START/PAUSE. Remove the basket and use silicone-tipped tongs to transfer the plantains, which should be tender, to a cutting board. Use the bottom of a heavy glass to smash each plantain flat. Spray both sides with cooking spray and place them back in the basket. Reinsert the basket and press START/PAUSE to resume cooking.
11. When the Zone 1 timer reads 5 minutes, press START/PAUSE. Remove the basket. Spoon half of the mojo sauce over the tilapia. Reinsert the basket and press START/PAUSE to resume cooking.
12. When cooking is complete, the fish should be cooked through and the plantains crispy. Serve the tilapia and plantains with the remaining mojo sauce for dipping.

Nutrition:
- (Per serving) Calories: 380; Total fat: 21g; Saturated fat: 2g; Carbohydrates: 20g; Fiber: 1g; Protein: 35g; Sodium: 217mg

Keto Baked Salmon With Pesto

Servings:2
Cooking Time:18
Ingredients:
- 4 salmon fillets, 2 inches thick
- 2 ounces green pesto
- Salt and black pepper
- ½ tablespoon of canola oil, for greasing
- 1-1/2 cup mayonnaise
- 2 tablespoons Greek yogurt
- Salt and black pepper, to taste

Directions:
1. Rub the salmon with pesto, salt, oil, and black pepper.
2. In a small bowl, whisk together all the green sauce ingredients.
3. Divide the fish fillets between both the baskets.
4. Set zone 1 to air fry mode for 18 minutes at 390 degrees F.
5. Select MATCH button for Zone 2 basket.
6. Once the cooking is done, serve it with green sauce drizzle.
7. Enjoy.

Nutrition:
- (Per serving) Calories 1165 | Fat80.7 g| Sodium 1087 mg | Carbs 33.1g | Fiber 0.5g | Sugar11.5 g | Protein 80.6g

Blackened Mahimahi With Honey-roasted Carrots

Servings:4

Cooking Time: 30 Minutes

Ingredients:

- FOR THE MAHIMAHI
- 4 mahimahi fillets (4 ounces each)
- 1 tablespoon olive oil
- 1 tablespoon blackening seasoning
- Lemon wedges, for serving
- FOR THE CARROTS
- 1 pound carrots, peeled and cut into ½-inch rounds
- 2 teaspoons vegetable oil
- ½ teaspoon kosher salt
- ¼ teaspoon freshly ground black pepper
- 1 tablespoon salted butter, cut into small pieces
- 1 tablespoon honey
- 2 tablespoons chopped fresh parsley

Directions:

1. To prep the mahimahi: Brush both sides of the fish with the oil and sprinkle with the blackening seasoning.

2. To prep the carrots: In a large bowl, combine the carrots, oil, salt, and black pepper. Stir well to coat the carrots with the oil.

3. To cook the mahimahi and carrots: Install a crisper plate in each of the two baskets. Place the fish in the Zone 1 basket and insert the basket in the unit. Place the carrots in the Zone 2 basket and insert the basket in the unit.

4. Select Zone 1, select AIR FRY, set the temperature to 380°F, and set the timer to 14 minutes.

5. Select Zone 2, select ROAST, set the temperature to 400°F, and set the timer to 30 minutes. Select SMART FINISH.

6. Press START/PAUSE to begin cooking.

7. When the Zone 2 timer reads 15 minutes, press START/PAUSE. Remove the basket and scatter the butter over the carrots, then drizzle them with the honey. Reinsert the basket and press START/PAUSE to resume cooking.

8. When cooking is complete, the fish should be cooked through and the carrots soft.

9. Stir the parsley into the carrots. Serve the fish with lemon wedges.

Nutrition:

- (Per serving) Calories: 235; Total fat: 9.5g; Saturated fat: 3g; Carbohydrates: 15g; Fiber: 3g; Protein: 22g; Sodium: 672mg

Steamed Cod With Garlic And Swiss Chard

Servings: 4

Cooking Time: 12 Minutes

Ingredients:

- 1 teaspoon salt
- ½ teaspoon dried oregano
- ½ teaspoon dried thyme
- ½ teaspoon garlic powder
- 4 cod fillets
- ½ white onion, thinly sliced
- 135 g Swiss chard, washed, stemmed, and torn into pieces
- 60 ml olive oil
- 1 lemon, quartered

Directions:

1. Preheat the air fryer to 192°C.

2. In a small bowl, whisk together the salt, oregano, thyme, and garlic powder.

3. Tear off four pieces of aluminum foil, with each sheet being large enough to envelop one cod fillet and a quarter of the vegetables.

4. Place a cod fillet in the middle of each sheet of foil, then sprinkle on all sides with the spice mixture.

5. In each foil packet, place a quarter of the onion slices and 30 g Swiss chard, then drizzle 1 tablespoon olive oil and squeeze ¼ lemon over the contents of each foil packet.

6. Fold and seal the sides of the foil packets and then place them into the two air fryer drawers. Steam for 12 minutes.

7. Remove from the drawers, and carefully open each packet to avoid a steam burn.

Orange-mustard Glazed Salmon And Cucumber And Salmon Salad

Servings: 4
Cooking Time: 10 Minutes
Ingredients:
- Orange-Mustard Glazed Salmon:
- 1 tablespoon orange marmalade
- ¼ teaspoon grated orange zest plus 1 tablespoon juice
- 2 teaspoons whole-grain mustard
- 2 (230 g) skin-on salmon fillets, 1½ inches thick
- Salt and pepper, to taste
- Vegetable oil spray
- Cucumber and Salmon Salad:
- 455 g salmon fillet
- 1½ tablespoons olive oil, divided
- 1 tablespoon sherry vinegar
- 1 tablespoon capers, rinsed and drained
- 1 seedless cucumber, thinly sliced
- ¼ white onion, thinly sliced
- 2 tablespoons chopped fresh parsley
- Salt and freshly ground black pepper, to taste

Directions:
1. Make the Orange-Mustard Glazed Salmon :
2. Preheat the air fryer to 205ºC.
3. Make foil sling for air fryer basket by folding 1 long sheet of aluminum foil so it is 4 inches wide. Lay sheet of foil widthwise across zone 1 basket, pressing foil into and up sides of basket. Fold excess foil as needed so that edges of foil are flush with top of basket. Lightly spray foil and basket with vegetable oil spray.
4. Combine marmalade, orange zest and juice, and mustard in bowl. Pat salmon dry with paper towels and season with salt and pepper. Brush tops and sides of fillets evenly with glaze. Arrange fillets skin side down on sling in prepared zone 1 basket, spaced evenly apart. Air fry salmon until center is still translucent when checked with the tip of a paring knife and registers 50ºC , 10 to 14 minutes, using sling to rotate fillets halfway through cooking.
5. Using the sling, carefully remove salmon from air fryer. Slide fish spatula along underside of fillets and transfer to individual serving plates, leaving skin behind. Serve.
6. Make the Cucumber and Salmon Salad :
7. Preheat the air fryer to 205ºC.
8. Lightly coat the salmon with ½ tablespoon of the olive oil. Place skin-side down in the zone 2 air fryer basket and air fry for 8 to 10 minutes until the fish is opaque and flakes easily with a fork. Transfer the salmon to a plate and let cool to room temperature. Remove the skin and carefully flake the fish into bite-size chunks.
9. In a small bowl, whisk the remaining 1 tablespoon olive oil and the vinegar until thoroughly combined. Add the flaked fish, capers, cucumber, onion, and parsley. Season to taste with salt and freshly ground black pepper. Toss gently to coat. Serve immediately or cover and refrigerate for up to 4 hours.

Crustless Prawn Quiche

Servings: 2
Cooking Time: 20 Minutes
Ingredients:
- Vegetable oil
- 4 large eggs
- 120 ml single cream
- 110 g raw prawns, chopped
- 120 g shredded Parmesan or Swiss cheese
- 235 g chopped spring onions
- 1 teaspoon sweet smoked paprika
- 1 teaspoon Herbes de Provence
- 1 teaspoon black pepper
- ½ to 1 teaspoon kosher or coarse sea salt

Directions:
1. Generously grease a baking pan with vegetable oil.
2. In a large bowl, beat together the eggs and single cream. Add the prawns, 90 g of the cheese, the scallions, paprika, Herbes de Provence, pepper, and salt. Stir with a fork to thoroughly combine. Pour the egg mixture into the prepared pan.
3. Place the pan in the zone 1 air fryer basket. Set the air fryer to 150ºC for 20 minutes. After 17 minutes, sprinkle the remaining 30 g cheese on top and cook for the remaining 3 minutes, or until the cheese has melted, the eggs are set, and a toothpick inserted into the center comes out clean.
4. Serve the quiche warm or at room temperature.

Pecan-crusted Catfish Nuggets With "fried" Okra

Servings:4
Cooking Time: 17 Minutes
Ingredients:

- FOR THE CATFISH NUGGETS
- 1 cup whole milk
- 1 pound fresh catfish nuggets (or cut-up fillets)
- 1 large egg
- 2 to 3 dashes Louisiana-style hot sauce (optional)
- ¼ cup finely chopped pecans
- ½ cup all-purpose flour
- Nonstick cooking spray
- Tartar sauce, for serving (optional)
- FOR THE OKRA
- ½ cup fine yellow cornmeal
- ¼ cup all-purpose flour
- ½ teaspoon garlic powder
- ½ teaspoon paprika
- 1 teaspoon kosher salt
- 1 large egg
- 8 ounces frozen cut okra, thawed
- Nonstick cooking spray

Directions:

1. To prep the catfish: Pour the milk into a large zip-top bag. Add the catfish and turn to coat. Set in the refrigerator to soak for at least 1 hour or up to overnight.
2. Remove the fish from the milk, shaking off any excess liquid.
3. In a shallow dish, whisk together the egg and hot sauce (if using). In a second shallow dish, combine the pecans and flour.
4. Dip each piece of fish into the egg mixture, then into the nut mixture to coat. Gently press the nut mixture to adhere to the fish. Spritz each nugget with cooking spray.
5. To prep the okra: Set up a breading station with two small shallow bowls. In the first bowl, stir together the cornmeal, flour, garlic powder, paprika, and salt. In the second bowl, whisk the egg.
6. Dip the okra first in the cornmeal mixture, then the egg, then back into the cornmeal. Spritz with cooking spray.
7. To cook the catfish and okra: Install a crisper plate in each of the two baskets. Place the fish in a single layer in the Zone 1 basket and insert the basket in the unit. Place the okra in the Zone 2 basket and insert the basket in the unit.
8. Select Zone 1, select AIR FRY, set the temperature to 390°F, and set the timer to 17 minutes.
9. Select Zone 2, select AIR FRY, set the temperature to 400°F, and set the timer to 12 minutes. Select SMART FINISH.
10. Press START/PAUSE to begin cooking.
11. When cooking is complete, the fish should be cooked through and the okra golden brown and crispy. Serve hot.

Nutrition:

- (Per serving) Calories: 414; Total fat: 24g; Saturated fat: 2.5g; Carbohydrates: 30g; Fiber: 3g; Protein: 23g; Sodium: 569mg

Spicy Salmon Fillets

Servings: 6
Cooking Time: 8 Minutes
Ingredients:

- 900g salmon fillets
- ¾ tsp ground cumin
- 1 tbsp brown sugar
- 2 tbsp steak seasoning
- ¼ tsp cayenne pepper
- ½ tsp ground coriander

Directions:

1. Mix ground cumin, coriander, steak seasoning, brown sugar, and cayenne in a small bowl.
2. Rub salmon fillets with spice mixture.
3. Insert a crisper plate in the Tefal air fryer baskets.
4. Place the salmon fillets in both baskets.
5. Select zone 1, then select "bake" mode and set the temperature to 360 degrees F for 10 minutes. Press "match" to match zone 2 settings to zone 1. Press "start/stop" to begin.

Nutrition:

- (Per serving) Calories 207 | Fat 9.4g |Sodium 68mg | Carbs 1.6g | Fiber 0.1g | Sugar 1.5g | Protein 29.4g

Tasty Parmesan Shrimp

Servings: 6
Cooking Time: 10minutes
Ingredients:
- 908g cooked shrimp, peeled & deveined
- ½ tsp oregano
- 59g parmesan cheese, grated
- 1 tbsp garlic, minced
- 30ml olive oil
- 1 tsp onion powder
- 1 tsp basil
- Pepper
- Salt

Directions:
1. Toss shrimp with oregano, cheese, garlic, oil, onion powder, basil, pepper, and salt in a bowl.
2. Insert a crisper plate in the Tefal air fryer baskets.
3. Add the shrimp mixture to both baskets.
4. Select zone 1, then select "air fry" mode and set the temperature to 360 degrees F for 10 minutes. Press "match" to match zone 2 settings to zone 1. Press "start/stop" to begin.

Nutrition:
- (Per serving) Calories 224 | Fat 7.3g |Sodium 397mg | Carbs 3.2g | Fiber 0.1g | Sugar 0.2g | Protein 34.6g

Salmon With Cauliflower

Servings: 4
Cooking Time: 25 Minutes
Ingredients:
- 455 g salmon fillet, diced
- 100 g cauliflower, shredded
- 1 tablespoon dried coriander
- 1 tablespoon coconut oil, melted
- 1 teaspoon ground turmeric
- 60 ml coconut cream

Directions:
1. Mix salmon with cauliflower, dried cilantro, ground turmeric, coconut cream, and coconut oil.
2. Transfer the salmon mixture into the air fryer and cook the meal at 176ºC for 25 minutes. Stir the meal every 5 minutes to avoid the burning.

Lemon Butter Salmon

Servings: 2
Cooking Time:12 Minutes
Ingredients:
- 2 salmon fillets
- 1/2 tsp soy sauce
- 3/4 tsp dill, chopped
- 1 tsp garlic, minced
- 1 1/2 tbsp fresh lemon juice
- 2 tbsp butter, melted
- Pepper
- Salt

Directions:
1. Preheat the air fryer to 400 F.
2. In a small bowl, mix butter, lemon juice, garlic, dill, soy sauce, pepper, and salt.
3. Brush salmon fillets with butter mixture and place into the air fryer basket and cook for 10-12 minutes.
4. Pour the remaining butter mixture over cooked salmon fillets and serve.

Buttered Mahi-mahi

Servings: 4
Cooking Time: 22 Minutes
Ingredients:
- 4 (6-oz) mahi-mahi fillets
- Salt and black pepper ground to taste
- Cooking spray
- ⅔ cup butter

Directions:
1. Preheat your Tefal Dual Zone Air Fryer to 350 degrees F.
2. Rub the mahi-mahi fillets with salt and black pepper.
3. Place two mahi-mahi fillets in each of the crisper plate.
4. Return the crisper plates to the Tefal Dual Zone Air Fryer.
5. Choose the Air Fry mode for Zone 1 and set the temperature to 390 degrees F and the time to 17 minutes|
6. Select the "MATCH" button to copy the settings for Zone 2.
7. Initiate cooking by pressing the START/STOP button.
8. Add butter to a saucepan and cook for 5 minutes until slightly brown.
9. Remove the butter from the heat.
10. Drizzle butter over the fish and serve warm.

Crispy Parmesan Cod

Servings: 2
Cooking Time: 10 Minutes
Ingredients:

- 455g cod filets
- Salt and black pepper, to taste
- ½ cup flour
- 2 large eggs, beaten
- ½ teaspoon salt
- 1 cup Panko
- ½ cup grated parmesan
- 2 teaspoons old bay seasoning
- ½ teaspoon garlic powder
- Olive oil spray

Directions:

1. Rub the cod fillets with black pepper and salt.
2. Mix panko with parmesan cheese, old bay seasoning, and garlic powder in a bowl.
3. Mix flour with salt in another bowl.
4. Dredge the cod filets in the flour then dip in the eggs and coat with the Panko mixture.
5. Place the cod fillets in the air fryer baskets.
6. Return the air fryer basket 1 to Zone 1, and basket 2 to Zone 2 of the Tefal 2-Basket Air Fryer.
7. Choose the "Air Fry" mode for Zone 1 and set the temperature to 400 degrees F and 10 minutes of cooking time.
8. Select the "MATCH COOK" option to copy the settings for Zone 2.
9. Initiate cooking by pressing the START/PAUSE BUTTON.
10. Flip the cod fillets once cooked halfway through.
11. Serve warm.

Nutrition:

- (Per serving) Calories 275 | Fat 1.4g |Sodium 582mg | Carbs 31.5g | Fiber 1.1g | Sugar 0.1g | Protein 29.8g

Tuna-stuffed Quinoa Patties

Servings: 4
Cooking Time: 15 Minutes
Ingredients:

- 35 g quinoa
- 4 slices white bread with crusts removed
- 120 ml milk
- 3 eggs
- 280 g tuna packed in olive oil, drained
- 2 to 3 lemons
- Kosher or coarse sea salt, and pepper, to taste
- 150 g panko bread crumbs
- Vegetable oil, for spraying
- Lemon wedges, for serving

Directions:

1. Rinse the quinoa in a fine-mesh sieve until the water runs clear. Bring 1 liter of salted water to a boil. Add the quinoa, cover, and reduce heat to low. Simmer the quinoa covered until most of the water is absorbed and the quinoa is tender, 15 to 20 minutes. Drain and allow to cool to room temperature. Meanwhile, soak the bread in the milk.
2. Mix the drained quinoa with the soaked bread and 2 of the eggs in a large bowl and mix thoroughly. In a medium bowl, combine the tuna, the remaining egg, and the juice and zest of 1 of the lemons. Season well with salt and pepper. Spread the panko on a plate.
3. Scoop up approximately 60 g of the quinoa mixture and flatten into a patty. Place a heaping tablespoon of the tuna mixture in the center of the patty and close the quinoa around the tuna. Flatten the patty slightly to create an oval-shaped croquette. Dredge both sides of the croquette in the panko. Repeat with the remaining quinoa and tuna.
4. Spray the two air fryer baskets with oil to prevent sticking, and preheat the air fryer to 205°C. Arrange 4 or 5 of the croquettes in each basket, taking care to avoid overcrowding. Spray the tops of the croquettes with oil. Air fry for 8 minutes until the top side is browned and crispy. Carefully turn the croquettes over and spray the second side with oil. Air fry until the second side is browned and crispy, another 7 minutes.
5. Serve the croquetas warm with plenty of lemon wedges for spritzing.

Cod With Jalapeño

Servings: 4
Cooking Time: 14 Minutes
Ingredients:

- 4 cod fillets, boneless
- 1 jalapeño, minced
- 1 tablespoon avocado oil
- ½ teaspoon minced garlic

Directions:

1. In the shallow bowl, mix minced jalapeño, avocado oil, and minced garlic.
2. Put the cod fillets in the two air fryer drawers in one layer and top with minced jalapeño mixture.
3. Cook the fish at 185°C for 7 minutes per side.

Bacon-wrapped Shrimp

Servings: 8
Cooking Time: 10 Minutes
Ingredients:

- 24 jumbo raw shrimp, deveined with tail on, fresh or thawed from frozen
- 8 slices bacon, cut into thirds
- 1 tablespoon olive oil
- 1 teaspoon paprika
- 1–2 cloves minced garlic
- 1 tablespoon finely chopped fresh parsley

Directions:

1. Combine the olive oil, paprika, garlic, and parsley in a small bowl.
2. If necessary, peel the raw shrimp, leaving the tails on.
3. Add the shrimp to the oil mixture. Toss to coat well.
4. Wrap a piece of bacon around the middle of each shrimp and place seam-side down on a small baking dish.
5. Refrigerate for 30 minutes before cooking.
6. Place a crisper plate in each drawer. Put the shrimp in a single layer in each drawer. Insert the drawers into the unit.
7. Select zone 1, then AIR FRY, then set the temperature to 360 degrees F/ 180 degrees C with a 10-minute timer. To match zone 2 settings to zone 1, choose MATCH. To begin, select START/STOP.
8. Remove the shrimp from the drawers when the cooking time is over.

Nutrition:

- (Per serving) Calories 479 | Fat 15.7g | Sodium 949mg | Carbs 0.6g | Fiber 0.1g | Sugar 0g | Protein 76.1g

Salmon With Fennel Salad

Servings: 4
Cooking Time: 17 Minutes
Ingredients:

- 2 teaspoons fresh parsley, chopped
- 1 teaspoon fresh thyme, chopped
- 1 teaspoon salt
- 4 (6-oz) skinless center-cut salmon fillets
- 2 tablespoons olive oil
- 4 cups fennel, sliced
- ⅔ cup Greek yogurt
- 1 garlic clove, grated
- 2 tablespoons orange juice
- 1 teaspoon lemon juice
- 2 tablespoons fresh dill, chopped

Directions:

1. Preheat your Tefal Dual Zone Air Fryer to 200 degrees F.
2. Mix ½ teaspoon of salt, thyme, and parsley in a small bowl.
3. Brush the salmon with oil first, then rub liberally rub the herb mixture.
4. Place 2 salmon fillets in each of the crisper plate.
5. Return the crisper plate to the Tefal Dual Zone Air Fryer.
6. Choose the Air Fry mode for Zone 1 and set the temperature to 390 degrees F and the time to 17 minutes|
7. Select the "MATCH" button to copy the settings for Zone 2.
8. Initiate cooking by pressing the START/STOP button.
9. Meanwhile, mix fennel with garlic, yogurt, lemon juice, orange juice, remaining salt, and dill in a mixing bowl.
10. Serve the air fried salmon fillets with fennel salad.
11. Enjoy.

Healthy Lobster Cakes

Servings: 6
Cooking Time: 12 Minutes
Ingredients:

- 1 egg
- 145g cooked lobster meat
- 60g butter, melted
- 1 tbsp Cajun seasoning
- 50g breadcrumbs
- Pepper
- Salt

Directions:

1. In a shallow dish, add breadcrumbs, pepper, and salt.
2. In a bowl, mix lobster meat, Cajun seasoning, egg, and butter until well combined.
3. Make patties from the lobster meat mixture and coat with breadcrumbs.
4. Insert a crisper plate in the Tefal air fryer baskets.
5. Place the coated patties in both baskets.
6. Select zone 1, then select "bake" mode and set the temperature to 390 degrees F for 12 minutes. Press "match" to match zone 2 settings to zone 1. Press "start/stop" to begin.

Nutrition:

- (Per serving) Calories 119 | Fat 7.2g |Sodium 287mg | Carbs 6.6g | Fiber 0.4g | Sugar 0.6g | Protein 6.8g

Spicy Fish Fillet With Onion Rings

Servings:1
Cooking Time:12
Ingredients:

- 300 grams of onion rings, frozen and packed
- 1 codfish fillet, 8 ounces
- Salt and black pepper, to taste
- 1 teaspoon of lemon juice
- oil spray, for greasing

Directions:

1. Put the frozen onion rings in zone 1 basket of the air fryer.
2. Next pat dry the fish fillets with a paper towel and season them with salt, black pepper, and lemon juice.
3. Grease the fillet with oil spray.
4. Put the fish in zone 2 basket.
5. Use MAX crisp for zone 1 at 240 degrees for 9 minutes.

6. Use MAX crisp for zone 2 basket and set it to 210 degrees for 12 minutes.
7. Press sync and press start.
8. Once done, serve hot.

Nutrition:

- (Per serving) Calories 666| Fat23.5g| Sodium 911mg | Carbs 82g | Fiber 8.8g | Sugar 17.4g | Protein 30.4g

Oyster Po'boy

Servings: 4
Cooking Time: 5 Minutes
Ingredients:

- 105 g plain flour
- 40 g yellow cornmeal
- 1 tablespoon Cajun seasoning
- 1 teaspoon salt
- 2 large eggs, beaten
- 1 teaspoon hot sauce
- 455 g pre-shucked oysters
- 1 (12-inch) French baguette, quartered and sliced horizontally
- Tartar Sauce, as needed
- 150 g shredded lettuce, divided
- 2 tomatoes, cut into slices
- Cooking spray

Directions:

1. In a shallow bowl, whisk the flour, cornmeal, Cajun seasoning, and salt until blended. In a second shallow bowl, whisk together the eggs and hot sauce.
2. One at a time, dip the oysters in the cornmeal mixture, the eggs, and again in the cornmeal, coating thoroughly.
3. Preheat the zone 1 air fryer drawer to 204°C. Line the zone 1 air fryer drawer with baking paper.
4. Place the oysters on the baking paper and spritz with oil.
5. Air fry for 2 minutes. Shake the drawer, spritz the oysters with oil, and air fry for 3 minutes more until lightly browned and crispy.
6. Spread each sandwich half with Tartar Sauce. Assemble the po'boys by layering each sandwich with fried oysters, ½ cup shredded lettuce, and 2 tomato slices.
7. Serve immediately.

Quick Easy Salmon

Servings: 4
Cooking Time:8 Minutes

Ingredients:

- 4 salmon fillets
- 1/2 tsp smoked paprika
- 1 tsp garlic powder
- 1 tbsp olive oil
- Pepper
- Salt

Directions:

1. Preheat the air fryer to 400 F.
2. Brush salmon fillets with oil and sprinkle with smoked paprika, garlic powder, pepper, and salt.
3. Place salmon fillets into the air fryer basket and cook for 8 minutes.
4. Serve and enjoy.

Fried Tilapia

Servings: 4
Cooking Time: 20 Minutes

Ingredients:

- 4 fresh tilapia fillets, approximately 6 ounces each
- 2 teaspoons olive oil
- 2 teaspoons chopped fresh chives
- 2 teaspoons chopped fresh parsley
- 1 teaspoon minced garlic
- Freshly ground pepper, to taste
- Salt to taste

Directions:

1. Pat the tilapia fillets dry with a paper towel.
2. Stir together the olive oil, chives, parsley, garlic, salt, and pepper in a small bowl.
3. Brush the mixture over the top of the tilapia fillets.
4. Place a crisper plate in each drawer. Add the fillets in a single layer to each drawer. Insert the drawers into the unit.
5. Select zone 1, then AIR FRY, then set the temperature to 360 degrees F/ 180 degrees C with a 20-minute timer. To match zone 2 settings to zone 1, choose MATCH. To begin, select START/STOP.
6. Remove the tilapia fillets from the drawers after the timer has finished.

Nutrition:

- (Per serving) Calories 140 | Fat 5.7g | Sodium 125mg | Carbs 1.5g | Fiber 0.4g | Sugar 0g | Protein 21.7g

Fish Cakes

Servings: 4
Cooking Time: 10 To 12 Minutes

Ingredients:

- 1 large russet potato, mashed
- 340 g cod or other white fish
- Salt and pepper, to taste
- Olive or vegetable oil for misting or cooking spray
- 1 large egg
- 50 g potato starch
- 60 g panko breadcrumbs
- 1 tablespoon fresh chopped chives
- 2 tablespoons minced onion

Directions:

1. Peel potatoes, cut into cubes, and cook on stovetop till soft.
2. Salt and pepper raw fish to taste. Mist with oil or cooking spray, and air fry at 182ºC for 6 to 8 minutes, until fish flakes easily. If fish is crowded, rearrange halfway through cooking to ensure all pieces cook evenly.
3. Transfer fish to a plate and break apart to cool.
4. Beat egg in a shallow dish.
5. Place potato starch in another shallow dish, and panko crumbs in a third dish.
6. When potatoes are done, drain in colander and rinse with cold water.
7. In a large bowl, mash the potatoes and stir in the chives and onion. Add salt and pepper to taste, then stir in the fish.
8. If needed, stir in a tablespoon of the beaten egg to help bind the mixture.
9. Shape into 8 small, fat patties. Dust lightly with potato starch, dip in egg, and roll in panko crumbs. Spray both sides with oil or cooking spray.
10. Air fry for 10 to 12 minutes, until golden brown and crispy.

Foil Packet Salmon

Servings: 4
Cooking Time: 14 Minutes
Ingredients:

- 455g salmon fillets
- 4 cups green beans defrosted
- 4 tablespoons soy sauce
- 2 tablespoons honey
- 2 teaspoons sesame seeds
- 1 teaspoon garlic powder
- ½ teaspoon ginger powder
- ½ teaspoon salt
- ¼ teaspoon white pepper
- ¼ teaspoon red pepper flakes
- Salt, to taste
- Canola oil spray

Directions:

1. Make 4 foil packets and adjust the salmon fillets in each.
2. Divide the green beans in the foil packets and drizzle half of the spices on top.
3. Place one salmon piece on top of each and drizzle the remaining ingredients on top.
4. Pack the salmon with the foil and place two packets in each air fryer basket.
5. Return the air fryer basket 1 to Zone 1, and basket 2 to Zone 2 of the Tefal 2-Basket Air Fryer.
6. Choose the "Air Fry" mode for Zone 1 and set the temperature to 425 degrees F and 14 minutes of cooking time.
7. Select the "MATCH COOK" option to copy the settings for Zone 2.
8. Initiate cooking by pressing the START/PAUSE BUTTON.
9. Serve warm.

Nutrition:

- (Per serving) Calories 305 | Fat 15g |Sodium 482mg | Carbs 17g | Fiber 3g | Sugar 2g | Protein 35g

"fried" Fish With Seasoned Potato Wedges

Servings:4
Cooking Time: 30 Minutes
Ingredients:

- FOR THE FISH
- 4 cod fillets (6 ounces each)
- 4 tablespoons all-purpose flour, divided
- ¼ cup cornstarch
- 1 teaspoon baking powder
- ¼ teaspoon kosher salt
- ⅓ cup lager-style beer or sparkling water
- Tartar sauce, cocktail sauce, or malt vinegar, for serving (optional)
- FOR THE POTATOES
- 4 russet potatoes
- 2 tablespoons vegetable oil
- ½ teaspoon paprika
- ½ teaspoon kosher salt
- ¼ teaspoon garlic powder
- ¼ teaspoon freshly ground black pepper

Directions:

1. To prep the fish: Pat the fish dry with a paper towel and coat lightly with 2 tablespoons of flour.
2. In a shallow dish, combine the remaining 2 tablespoons of flour, the cornstarch, baking powder, and salt. Stir in the beer to form a thick batter.
3. Dip the fish in the batter to coat both sides, then let rest on a cutting board for 10 minutes.
4. To prep the potatoes: Cut each potato in half lengthwise, then cut each half into 4 wedges.
5. In a large bowl, combine the potatoes and oil. Toss well to fully coat the potatoes. Add the paprika, salt, garlic powder, and black pepper and toss well to coat.
6. To cook the fish and potato wedges: Install a crisper plate in each of the two baskets. Place a piece of parchment paper or aluminum foil over the plate in the Zone 1 basket. Place the fish in the basket and insert the basket in the unit. Place the potato wedges in a single layer in the Zone 2 basket and insert the basket in the unit.
7. Select Zone 1, select AIR FRY, set the temperature to 400°F, and set the timer to 13 minutes.
8. Select Zone 2, select AIR FRY, set the temperature to 400°F, and set the timer to 30 minutes. Select SMART FINISH.
9. Press START/PAUSE to begin cooking.
10. When the Zone 1 timer reads 5 minutes, press START/PAUSE. Remove the basket and use a silicone spatula to carefully flip the fish over. Reinsert the basket and press START/PAUSE to resume cooking.
11. When cooking is complete, the fish should be cooked through and the potatoes crispy outside and tender inside. Serve hot with tartar sauce, cocktail sauce, or malt vinegar (if using).

Nutrition:

- (Per serving) Calories: 360; Total fat: 8g; Saturated fat: 1g; Carbohydrates: 40g; Fiber: 2g; Protein: 30g; Sodium: 302mg

Tuna Patties

Servings: 6
Cooking Time: 10 Minutes
Ingredients:
- For the tuna patties:
- 1 tablespoon extra-virgin olive oil
- 1 tablespoon butter
- ½ cup chopped onion
- ½ red bell pepper, chopped
- 1 teaspoon minced garlic
- 2 (7-ounce) cans or 3 (5-ounce) cans albacore tuna fish in water, drained
- 1 tablespoon lime juice
- 1 celery stalk, chopped
- ¼ cup chopped fresh parsley
- 3 tablespoons grated parmesan cheese
- ½ teaspoon dried oregano
- ¼ teaspoon salt
- Black pepper, to taste
- 1 teaspoon sriracha
- ½ cup panko crumbs
- 2 whisked eggs
- For the crumb coating:
- ½ cup panko crumbs
- ¼ cup parmesan cheese
- Non-stick spray

Directions:
1. In a skillet, heat the oil and butter over medium-high heat.
2. Sauté the onions, red bell pepper, and garlic for 5 to 7 minutes.
3. Drain the tuna from the cans thoroughly. Put the tuna in a large mixing bowl. Add the lime juice.
4. Add the sautéed vegetables to the mixing bowl.
5. Add the celery, parsley, and cheese. Combine well.
6. Add the oregano, salt, and pepper to taste. Mix well.
7. Add a dash of sriracha for a spicy kick and mix well.
8. Add the panko crumbs and mix well.
9. Mix in the eggs until the mixture is well combined. You can add an extra egg if necessary, but the tuna is usually wet enough that it isn't required. Form 6 patties from the mixture.
10. Refrigerate for 30 to 60 minutes (or even overnight).
11. Remove from refrigerator and coat with a mixture of the ½ cup of panko crumbs and ¼ cup of parmesan cheese.
12. Spray the tops of the coated patties with some non-stick cooking spray.
13. Place a crisper place in each drawer. Put 3 patties in each drawer. Insert the drawers into the unit.
14. Select zone 1, then AIR FRY, then set the temperature to 390 degrees F/ 200 degrees C with a 10-minute timer. To match zone 2 settings to zone 1, choose MATCH. To begin, select START/STOP.
15. Remove and garnish with chopped parsley.

Nutrition:
- (Per serving) Calories 381 | Fat 16g | Sodium 1007mg | Carbs 23g | Fiber 2g | Sugar 4g | Protein 38g

Shrimp Skewers

Servings: 4
Cooking Time: 10minutes
Ingredients:
- 453g shrimp
- 15ml lemon juice
- 15ml olive oil
- 1 tbsp old bay seasoning
- 1 tsp garlic, minced

Directions:
1. Toss shrimp with old bay seasoning, garlic, lemon juice, and olive oil in a bowl.
2. Thread shrimp onto the soaked skewers.
3. Insert a crisper plate in the Tefal air fryer baskets.
4. Place the shrimp skewers in both baskets.
5. Select zone 1, then select "air fry" mode and set the temperature to 390 degrees F for 10 minutes. Press "match" to match zone 2 settings to zone 1. Press "start/stop" to begin.

Nutrition:
- (Per serving) Calories 167 | Fat 5.5g |Sodium 758mg | Carbs 2g | Fiber 0g | Sugar 0.1g | Protein 25.9g

Breaded Scallops

Servings: 4

Cooking Time: 12 Minutes

Ingredients:

- ½ cup crushed buttery crackers
- ½ teaspoon garlic powder
- ½ teaspoon seafood seasoning
- 2 tablespoons butter, melted
- 1 pound sea scallops patted dry
- cooking spray

Directions:

1. Mix cracker crumbs, garlic powder, and seafood seasoning in a shallow bowl. Spread melted butter in another shallow bowl.

2. Dip each scallop in the melted butter and then roll in the breading to coat well.

3. Grease each Air fryer basket with cooking spray and place half of the scallops in each.

4. Return the crisper plate to the Tefal Dual Zone Air Fryer.

5. Select the Air Fry mode for Zone 1 and set the temperature to 390 degrees F and the time to 12 minutes|

6. Press the "MATCH" button to copy the settings for Zone 2.

7. Initiate cooking by pressing the START/STOP button.

8. Flip the scallops with a spatula after 4 minutes and resume cooking.

9. Serve warm.

Sweet & Spicy Fish Fillets

Servings: 4

Cooking Time: 8 Minutes

Ingredients:

- 4 salmon fillets
- 1 tsp smoked paprika
- 1 tsp chilli powder
- ½ tsp red pepper flakes, crushed
- ½ tsp garlic powder
- 85g honey
- Pepper
- Salt

Directions:

1. In a small bowl, mix honey, garlic powder, chilli powder, paprika, red pepper flakes, pepper, and salt.

2. Brush fish fillets with honey mixture.

3. Insert a crisper plate in the Tefal air fryer baskets.

4. Place fish fillets in both baskets.

5. Select zone 1, then select "air fry" mode and set the temperature to 390 degrees F for 8 minutes. Press "match" and then"start/stop" to begin.

Nutrition:

- (Per serving) Calories 305 | Fat 11.2g |Sodium 125mg | Carbs 18.4g | Fiber 0.6g | Sugar 17.5g | Protein 34.8g

Salmon With Broccoli And Cheese

Servings:2

Cooking Time:18

Ingredients:

- 2 cups of broccoli
- ½ cup of butter, melted
- Salt and pepper, to taste
- Oil spray, for greasing
- 1 cup of grated cheddar cheese
- 1 pound of salmon, fillets

Directions:

1. Take a bowl and add broccoli to it.

2. Add salt and black pepper and spray it with oil.

3. Put the broccoli in the air fryer zone 1 backset.

4. Now rub the salmon fillets with salt, black pepper, and butter.

5. Put it into zone 2 baskets.

6. Set zone 1 to air fry mode for 5 minters at 400 degrees F.

7. Set zone 2 to air fry mode for 18 minutes at 390 degrees F.

8. Hit start to start the cooking.

9. Once done, serve and by placing it on serving plates.

10. Put the grated cheese on top of the salmon and serve.

Nutrition:

- (Per serving) Calories 966 | Fat 79.1 g| Sodium 808 mg | Carbs 6.8 g | Fiber 2.4g | Sugar 1.9g | Protein 61.2 g

Blackened Red Snapper

Servings: 4
Cooking Time: 8 To 10 Minutes
Ingredients:

- 1½ teaspoons black pepper
- ¼ teaspoon thyme
- ¼ teaspoon garlic powder
- ⅛ teaspoon cayenne pepper
- 1 teaspoon olive oil
- 4 red snapper fillet portions, skin on, 110 g each
- 4 thin slices lemon
- Cooking spray

Directions:

1. Mix the spices and oil together to make a paste. Rub into both sides of the fish.
2. Spray the two air fryer drawers with nonstick cooking spray and lay snapper steaks in drawers, skin-side down.
3. Place a lemon slice on each piece of fish.
4. Roast at 200ºC for 8 to 10 minutes. The fish will not flake when done, but it should be white through the center.

Sole And Cauliflower Fritters And Prawn Bake

Servings: 6
Cooking Time: 24 Minutes
Ingredients:

- Sole and Cauliflower Fritters:
- 230 g sole fillets
- 230 g mashed cauliflower
- 75 g red onion, chopped
- 1 bell pepper, finely chopped
- 1 egg, beaten
- 2 garlic cloves, minced
- 2 tablespoons fresh parsley, chopped
- 1 tablespoon olive oil
- 1 tablespoon coconut aminos or tamari
- ½ teaspoon scotch bonnet pepper, minced
- ½ teaspoon paprika
- Salt and white pepper, to taste
- Cooking spray
- Prawn Bake:
- 400 g prawns, peeled and deveined
- 1 egg, beaten
- 120 ml coconut milk
- 120 g Cheddar cheese, shredded

- ½ teaspoon coconut oil
- 1 teaspoon ground coriander

Directions:

1. Make the Sole and Cauliflower Fritters :
2. 1. Preheat the air fryer to 200ºC. Spray the zone 1 air fryer basket with cooking spray. Place the sole fillets in the basket and air fry for 10 minutes, flipping them halfway through. 3. When the fillets are done, transfer them to a large bowl. Mash the fillets into flakes. Add the remaining ingredients and stir to combine. 4. Make the fritters: Scoop out 2 tablespoons of the fish mixture and shape into a patty about ½ inch thick with your hands. Repeat with the remaining fish mixture. 5. Arrange the patties in the zone 1 air fryer basket and bake for 14 minutes, flipping the patties halfway through, or until they are golden brown and cooked through. 6. Cool for 5 minutes and serve on a plate.
3. Make the Prawn Bake :
4. In the mixing bowl, mix prawns with egg, coconut milk, Cheddar cheese, coconut oil, and ground coriander.
5. Then put the mixture in the baking ramekins and put in the zone 2 air fryer basket.
6. Cook the prawns at 205ºC for 5 minutes.

Easy Herbed Salmon

Servings: 2
Cooking Time:5 Minutes
Ingredients:

- 2 salmon fillets
- 1 tbsp butter
- 2 tbsp olive oil
- 1/4 tsp paprika
- 1 tsp herb de Provence
- Pepper
- Salt

Directions:

1. Brush salmon fillets with oil and sprinkle with paprika, herb de Provence, pepper, and salt.
2. Place salmon fillets into the air fryer basket and cook at 390 F for 5 minutes.
3. Melt butter in a pan and pour over cooked salmon fillets.
4. Serve and enjoy.

Crumb-topped Sole

Servings: 4

Cooking Time: 7 Minutes

Ingredients:

- 3 tablespoons mayonnaise
- 3 tablespoons Parmesan cheese, grated
- 2 teaspoons mustard seeds
- ¼ teaspoon black pepper
- 4 (170g) sole fillets
- 1 cup soft bread crumbs
- 1 green onion, chopped
- ½ teaspoon ground mustard
- 2 teaspoons butter, melted
- Cooking spray

Directions:

1. Mix mayonnaise with black pepper, mustard seeds, and 2 tablespoons cheese in a bowl.
2. Place 2 sole fillets in each air fryer basket and top them with mayo mixture.
3. Mix breadcrumbs with rest of the ingredients in a bowl.
4. Drizzle this mixture over the sole fillets.
5. Return the air fryer basket 1 to Zone 1, and basket 2 to Zone 2 of the Tefal 2-Basket Air Fryer.
6. Choose the "Air Fry" mode for Zone 1 and set the temperature to 375 degrees F and 7 minutes of cooking time.
7. Select the "MATCH COOK" option to copy the settings for Zone 2.
8. Initiate cooking by pressing the START/PAUSE BUTTON.
9. Serve warm.

Nutrition:

- (Per serving) Calories 308 | Fat 24g |Sodium 715mg | Carbs 0.8g | Fiber 0.1g | Sugar 0.1g | Protein 21.9g

Pretzel-crusted Catfish

Servings: 4

Cooking Time: 12 Minutes

Ingredients:

- 4 catfish fillets
- ½ teaspoon salt
- ½ teaspoon black pepper
- 2 large eggs
- ⅓ cup Dijon mustard
- 2 tablespoons 2% milk
- ½ cup all-purpose flour
- 4 cups miniature pretzels, crushed
- Cooking spray
- Lemon slices

Directions:

1. Rub the catfish with black pepper and salt.
2. Beat eggs with milk and mustard in a bowl.
3. Spread pretzels and flour in two separate bowls.
4. Coat the catfish with flour then dip in the egg mixture and coat with the pretzels.
5. Place two fish fillets in each air fryer basket.
6. Return the air fryer basket 1 to Zone 1, and basket 2 to Zone 2 of the Tefal 2-Basket Air Fryer.
7. Choose the "Air Fry" mode for Zone 1 at 325 degrees F and 12 minutes of cooking time.
8. Select the "MATCH COOK" option to copy the settings for Zone 2.
9. Initiate cooking by pressing the START/PAUSE BUTTON.
10. Serve warm.

Nutrition:

- (Per serving) Calories 196 | Fat 7.1g |Sodium 492mg | Carbs 21.6g | Fiber 2.9g | Sugar 0.8g | Protein 13.4g

Parmesan Wings

Servings: 4
Cooking Time: 30 Minutes
Ingredients:

- 900g chicken wings
- 1 tablespoon olive oil
- 1 tablespoon baking powder
- ½ teaspoon salt
- ½ teaspoon garlic powder
- ½ teaspoon onion powder
- ¼ teaspoon paprika
- ¼ teaspoon black pepper
- 5 tablespoons unsalted butter, melted
- 4-5 cloves garlic, minced
- 25g grated parmesan cheese

Directions:

1. Using paper towels, fully dry the wings and lay them in a large mixing bowl. Toss them in olive oil and toss to coat.
2. Combine the baking powder, salt, garlic powder, onion powder, paprika, and pepper in a small bowl. Toss the wings in the mixture to evenly coat them.
3. Press your chosen zone - "Zone 1" or "Zone 2" and then rotate the knob to select "Air Fry".
4. Set the temperature to 200 degrees C, and then set the time for 5 minutes to preheat.
5. After preheating, spray the Air-Fryer basket of each zone with cooking spray, arrange wings in a single layer, and spritz them with cooking spray.
6. Slide the basket into the Air Fryer and set the time for 15 minutes.
7. Carefully flip the wings and cook for 5 to 8 more minutes.
8. Meanwhile, in a microwave-safe bowl, melt the butter. Combine the minced garlic and parmesan cheese in a mixing bowl.
9. After cooking time is completed, combine with the garlic butter in a large mixing dish and serve on a serving plate.

Bacon-wrapped Dates Bacon-wrapped Scallops

Servings:6
Cooking Time: 12 Minutes
Ingredients:

- FOR THE SCALLOPS
- 6 slices bacon, halved crosswise
- 12 large sea scallops, patted dry
- FOR THE DATES
- 4 slices bacon, cut into thirds
- 12 pitted dates

Directions:

1. To prep the dates: Wrap each piece of bacon around a date and secure with a toothpick.
2. To cook the dates and the bacon for the scallops: Install a crisper plate in each of the two baskets. Place the bacon for the scallops in the Zone 1 basket in a single layer and insert the basket in the unit. Place the bacon-wrapped dates in the Zone 2 basket in a single layer and insert the basket in the unit.
3. Select Zone 1, select AIR FRY, set the temperature to 400°F, and set the time to 12 minutes.
4. Select Zone 2, select AIR FRY, set the temperature to 360°F, and set the time to 10 minutes. Select SMART FINISH.
5. Press START/PAUSE to begin cooking.
6. When the Zone 1 timer reads 9 minutes, press START/PAUSE. Remove the basket from the unit. Wrap each piece of bacon around a scallop and secure with a toothpick. Place the bacon-wrapped scallops in the basket. Reinsert the basket and press START/PAUSE to resume cooking.
7. When the Zone 1 timer reads 4 minutes, press START/PAUSE. Remove the basket and use silicone-tipped tongs to flip the scallops. Reinsert the basket and press START/PAUSE to resume cooking.
8. When cooking is complete, the scallops will be opaque and the bacon around both the scallops and dates will be crisp. Arrange the bacon-wrapped scallops and dates on a serving platter. Serve warm.

Nutrition:

- (Per serving) Calories: 191; Total fat: 2.5g; Saturated fat: 1g; Carbohydrates: 39g; Fiber: 4g; Protein: 3g; Sodium: 115mg

Jalapeño Poppers And Greek Potato Skins With Olives And Feta

Servings: 8
Cooking Time: 45 Minutes
Ingredients:

- Jalapeño Poppers:
- Oil, for spraying
- 227 g soft white cheese
- 177 ml gluten-free breadcrumbs, divided
- 2 tablespoons chopped fresh parsley
- ½ teaspoon granulated garlic
- ½ teaspoon salt
- 10 jalapeño peppers, halved and seeded
- Greek Potato Skins with Olives and Feta:
- 2 russet or Maris Piper potatoes
- 3 tablespoons olive oil, divided, plus more for drizzling (optional)
- 1 teaspoon rock salt, divided
- ¼ teaspoon black pepper
- 2 tablespoons fresh coriander, chopped, plus more for serving
- 60 ml Kalamata olives, diced
- 60 ml crumbled feta
- Chopped fresh parsley, for garnish (optional)

Directions:

1. Make the Jalapeño Popper s: Line the zone 1 air fryer basket with parchment and spray lightly with oil.
2. In a medium bowl, mix together the soft white cheese, half of the breadcrumbs, the parsley, garlic, and salt. 3. Spoon the mixture into the jalapeño halves. Gently press the stuffed jalapeños in the remaining breadcrumbs. 4. Place the stuffed jalapeños in the prepared basket. 5. Air fry at 190°C for 20 minutes, or until the cheese is melted and the breadcrumbs are crisp and golden brown.
2. Make the Greek Potato Skins with Olives and Feta :
3. Preheat the air fryer to 190°C.
4. Using a fork, poke 2 to 3 holes in the potatoes, then coat each with about ½ tablespoon olive oil and ½ teaspoon salt.
5. Place the potatoes into the zone 2 air fryer basket and bake for 30 minutes.
6. Remove the potatoes from the air fryer, and slice in half. Using a spoon, scoop out the flesh of the potatoes, leaving a ½-inch layer of potato inside the skins, and set the skins aside.

7. In a medium bowl, combine the scooped potato middles with the remaining 2 tablespoons of olive oil, ½ teaspoon of salt, black pepper, and coriander. Mix until well combined.
8. Divide the potato filling into the now-empty potato skins, spreading it evenly over them. Top each potato with a tablespoon each of the olives and feta.
9. Place the loaded potato skins back into the air fryer and bake for 15 minutes.
10. Serve with additional chopped coriander or parsley and a drizzle of olive oil, if desired.

Bruschetta With Basil Pesto

Servings: 4
Cooking Time: 5 To 11 Minutes
Ingredients:

- 8 slices French bread, ½ inch thick
- 2 tablespoons softened butter
- 240 ml shredded Mozzarella cheese
- 120 ml basil pesto
- 240 ml chopped grape tomatoes
- 2 spring onions, thinly sliced

Directions:

1. Preheat the air fryer to 175°C.
2. Spread the bread with the butter and place butter-side up in the two air fryer baskets. Bake for 3 to 5 minutes, or until the bread is light golden brown.
3. Remove the bread from the baskets and top each piece with some of the cheese. Return to the baskets in 2 baskets and bake for 1 to 3 minutes, or until the cheese melts.
4. Meanwhile, combine the pesto, tomatoes, and spring onions in a small bowl.
5. When the cheese has melted, remove the bread from the air fryer and place on a serving plate. Top each slice with some of the pesto mixture and serve.

Chicken Crescent Wraps

Servings: 6
Cooking Time: 12 Minutes.
Ingredients:
- 3 tablespoons chopped onion
- 3 garlic cloves, peeled and minced
- ¾ (8 ounces) package cream cheese
- 6 tablespoons butter
- 2 boneless chicken breasts, cubed, cooked
- 3 (10 ounces) cans refrigerated crescent roll dough

Directions:
1. Heat oil in a skillet and add onion and garlic to sauté until soft.
2. Add cooked chicken, sautéed veggies, butter, and cream cheese to a blender.
3. Blend well until smooth. Spread the crescent dough over a flat surface.
4. Slice the dough into 12 rectangles.
5. Spoon the chicken mixture at the center of each rectangle.
6. Roll the dough to wrap the mixture and form a ball.
7. Divide these balls into the two crisper plate.
8. Return the crisper plate to the Tefal Dual Zone Air Fryer.
9. Choose the Air Fry mode for Zone 1 and set the temperature to 390 degrees F and the time to 12 minutes.
10. Select the "MATCH" button to copy the settings for Zone 2.
11. Initiate cooking by pressing the START/STOP button.
12. Serve warm.

Nutrition:
- (Per serving) Calories 100 | Fat 2g |Sodium 480mg | Carbs 4g | Fiber 2g | Sugar 0g | Protein 18g

Bacon Wrapped Tater Tots

Servings: 8
Cooking Time: 15 Minutes
Ingredients:
- 8 bacon slices
- 3 tablespoons honey
- ½ tablespoon chipotle chile powder
- 16 frozen tater tots

Directions:
1. Cut the bacon slices in half and wrap each tater tot with a bacon slice.
2. Brush the bacon with honey and drizzle chipotle chile powder over them.
3. Insert a toothpick to seal the bacon.
4. Place the wrapped tots in the air fryer baskets.
5. Return the air fryer basket 1 to Zone 1, and basket 2 to Zone 2 of the Tefal 2-Basket Air Fryer.
6. Choose the "Air Fry" mode for Zone 1 at 350 degrees F and 14 minutes of cooking time.
7. Select the "MATCH COOK" option to copy the settings for Zone 2.
8. Initiate cooking by pressing the START/PAUSE BUTTON.
9. Serve warm.

Fried Ravioli

Servings: 6
Cooking Time: 10 Minutes
Ingredients:
- 12 frozen raviolis
- 118ml buttermilk
- ½ cup Italian breadcrumbs

Directions:
1. Dip the ravioli in the buttermilk then coat with the breadcrumbs.
2. Divide the ravioli into the Tefal 2 Baskets Air Fryer baskets.
3. Return the air fryer basket 1 to Zone 1, and basket 2 to Zone 2 of the Tefal 2-Basket Air Fryer.
4. Choose the "Air Fry" mode for Zone 1 and set the temperature to 400 degrees F and 7 minutes of cooking time.
5. Select the "MATCH COOK" option to copy the settings for Zone 2.
6. Initiate cooking by pressing the START/PAUSE BUTTON.
7. Flip the ravioli once cooked halfway through.
8. Serve warm.

Crunchy Basil White Beans And Artichoke And Olive Pitta Flatbread

Servings: 6
Cooking Time: 19 Minutes
Ingredients:

- Crunchy Basil White Beans:
- 1 (425 g) can cooked white beans
- 2 tablespoons olive oil
- 1 teaspoon fresh sage, chopped
- ¼ teaspoon garlic powder
- ¼ teaspoon salt, divided
- 1 teaspoon chopped fresh basil
- Artichoke and Olive Pitta Flatbread:
- 2 wholewheat pittas
- 2 tablespoons olive oil, divided
- 2 garlic cloves, minced
- ¼ teaspoon salt
- 120 ml canned artichoke hearts, sliced
- 60 ml Kalamata olives
- 60 ml shredded Parmesan
- 60 ml crumbled feta
- Chopped fresh parsley, for garnish (optional)

Directions:

1. Make the Crunchy Basil White Beans :
2. Preheat the air fryer to 190ºC.
3. In a medium bowl, mix together the beans, olive oil, sage, garlic, ⅛ teaspoon salt, and basil.
4. Pour the white beans into the air fryer and spread them out in a single layer.
5. Bake in zone 1 basket for 10 minutes. Stir and continue cooking for an additional 5 to 9 minutes, or until they reach your preferred level of crispiness.
6. Toss with the remaining ⅛ teaspoon salt before serving.
7. Make the Artichoke and Olive Pitta Flatbread :
8. Preheat the air fryer to 190ºC.
9. Brush each pitta with 1 tablespoon olive oil, then sprinkle the minced garlic and salt over the top.
10. Distribute the artichoke hearts, olives, and cheeses evenly between the two pittas, and place both into the zone 2 air fryer basket to bake for 10 minutes.
11. Remove the pittas and cut them into 4 pieces each before serving. Sprinkle parsley over the top, if desired.

Kale Potato Nuggets

Servings: 4
Cooking Time: 15 Minutes

Ingredients:

- 279g potatoes, chopped, boiled & mashed
- 268g kale, chopped
- 1 garlic clove, minced
- 30ml milk
- Pepper
- Salt

Directions:

1. In a bowl, mix potatoes, kale, milk, garlic, pepper, and salt until well combined.
2. Insert a crisper plate in the Tefal air fryer baskets.
3. Make small balls from the potato mixture and place them both baskets.
4. Select zone 1 then select "air fry" mode and set the temperature to 390 degrees F for 15 minutes. Press "match" to match zone 2 settings to zone 1. Press "start/stop" to begin. Turn halfway through.

Crispy Filo Artichoke Triangles

Servings: 18 Triangles
Cooking Time: 9 To 12 Minutes

Ingredients:

- 60 ml Ricotta cheese
- 1 egg white
- 80 ml minced and drained artichoke hearts
- 3 tablespoons grated Mozzarella cheese
- ½ teaspoon dried thyme
- 6 sheets frozen filo pastry, thawed
- 2 tablespoons melted butter

Directions:

1. Preheat the air fryer to 205ºC.
2. In a small bowl, combine the Ricotta cheese, egg white, artichoke hearts, Mozzarella cheese, and thyme, and mix well.
3. Cover the filo pastry with a damp kitchen towel while you work so it doesn't dry out. Using one sheet at a time, place on the work surface and cut into thirds lengthwise.
4. Put about 1½ teaspoons of the filling on each strip at the base. Fold the bottom right-hand tip of phyllo over the filling to meet the other side in a triangle, then continue folding in a triangle. Brush each triangle with butter to seal the edges. Repeat with the remaining phyllo dough and filling.
5. Place the triangles in the two air fryer baskets. Bake, 6 at a time, in two baskets for about 3 to 4 minutes, or until the filo is golden brown and crisp.
6. Serve hot.

Dried Apple Chips Dried Banana Chips

Servings:6
Cooking Time: 6 To 10 Hours
Ingredients:
- FOR THE APPLE CHIPS
- ½ teaspoon ground cinnamon
- ¼ teaspoon ground nutmeg
- ⅛ teaspoon ground allspice
- ⅛ teaspoon ground ginger
- 2 Gala apples, cored and cut into ⅛-inch-thick rings
- FOR THE BANANA CHIPS
- 2 firm-ripe bananas, cut into ¼-inch slices

Directions:
1. To prep the apple chips: In a small bowl, mix the cinnamon, nutmeg, allspice, and ginger until combined. Sprinkle the spice mixture over the apple slices.
2. To dehydrate the fruit: Arrange half of the apple slices in a single layer in the Zone 1 basket. It is okay if the edges overlap a bit as they will shrink as they cook. Place a crisper plate on top of the apples. Arrange the remaining apple slices on top of the crisper plate and insert the basket in the unit.
3. Repeat this process with the bananas in the Zone 2 basket and insert the basket in the unit.
4. Select Zone 1, select DEHYDRATE, set the temperature to 135°F, and set the time to 8 hours.
5. Select Zone 2, select DEHYDRATE, set the temperature to 135°F, and set the time to 10 hours. Select SMART FINISH.
6. Press START/PAUSE to begin cooking.
7. When both timers read 2 hours, press START/PAUSE. Remove both baskets and check the fruit for doneness; note that juicier fruit will take longer to dry than fruit that starts out drier. Reinsert the basket and press START/PAUSE to continue cooking if necessary.

Nutrition:
- (Per serving) Calories: 67; Total fat: 0g; Saturated fat: 0g; Carbohydrates: 16g; Fiber: 3g; Protein: 0g; Sodium: 1mg

Garlic Bread

Servings: 8
Cooking Time: 10 Minutes
Ingredients:
- 60g butter, softened
- 3 tablespoons grated Parmesan cheese
- 2 garlic cloves, minced
- 2 teaspoons minced fresh parsley
- 8 slices of French bread

Directions:
1. Press either "Zone 1" or "Zone 2" and then rotate the knob to select "Bake".
2. Set the temperature to 175 degrees C, and then set the time for 5 minutes to preheat.
3. After preheating, combine the first four ingredients in a small mixing bowl| spread on bread. Arrange bread slices onto basket.
4. Slide the basket into the Air Fryer and set the time for 3 minutes.
5. After cooking time is completed, transfer them onto serving plates and serve.

Fried Halloumi Cheese

Servings: 6
Cooking Time: 12 Minutes.
Ingredients:
- 1 block of halloumi cheese, sliced
- 2 teaspoons olive oil

Directions:
1. Divide the halloumi cheese slices in the crisper plate.
2. Drizzle olive oil over the cheese slices.
3. Return the crisper plate to the Tefal Dual Zone Air Fryer.
4. Choose the Air Fry mode for Zone 1 and set the temperature to 360 degrees F and the time to 12 minutes.
5. Flip the cheese slices once cooked halfway through.
6. Serve.

Nutrition:
- (Per serving) Calories 186 | Fat 3g |Sodium 223mg | Carbs 31g | Fiber 8.7g | Sugar 5.5g | Protein 9.7g

Onion Pakoras

Servings: 2
Cooking Time: 10 Minutes
Ingredients:

- 2 medium brown or white onions, sliced (475 ml)
- 120 ml chopped fresh coriander
- 2 tablespoons vegetable oil
- 1 tablespoon chickpea flour
- 1 tablespoon rice flour, or 2 tablespoons chickpea flour
- 1 teaspoon ground turmeric
- 1 teaspoon cumin seeds
- 1 teaspoon rock salt
- ½ teaspoon cayenne pepper
- Vegetable oil spray

Directions:

1. In a large bowl, combine the onions, coriander, oil, chickpea flour, rice flour, turmeric, cumin seeds, salt, and cayenne. Stir to combine. Cover and let stand for 30 minutes or up to overnight. Mix well before using.
2. Spray the air fryer baskets generously with vegetable oil spray. Drop the batter in 6 heaping tablespoons into the two baskets. Set the air fryer to 175°C for 8 minutes. Carefully turn the pakoras over and spray with oil spray. Set the air fryer for 2 minutes, or until the batter is cooked through and crisp, checking at 6 minutes for doneness. Serve hot.

Chicken Stuffed Mushrooms

Servings: 6
Cooking Time: 15 Minutes.
Ingredients:

- 6 large fresh mushrooms, stems removed
- Stuffing:
- ½ cup chicken meat, cubed
- 1 (4 ounces) package cream cheese, softened
- ¼ lb. imitation crabmeat, flaked
- 1 cup butter
- 1 garlic clove, peeled and minced
- Black pepper and salt to taste
- Garlic powder to taste
- Crushed red pepper to taste

Directions:

1. Melt and heat butter in a skillet over medium heat.
2. Add chicken and sauté for 5 minutes.
3. Add in all the remaining ingredients for the stuffing.
4. Cook for 5 minutes, then turn off the heat.

5. Allow the mixture to cool. Stuff each mushroom with a tablespoon of this mixture.
6. Divide the stuffed mushrooms in the two crisper plates.
7. Return the crisper plate to the Tefal Dual Zone Air Fryer.
8. Choose the Air Fry mode for Zone 1 and set the temperature to 375 degrees F and the time to 15 minutes.
9. Select the "MATCH" button to copy the settings for Zone 2.
10. Initiate cooking by pressing the START/STOP button.
11. Serve warm.

Nutrition:

- (Per serving) Calories 180 | Fat 3.2g |Sodium 133mg | Carbs 32g | Fiber 1.1g | Sugar 1.8g | Protein 9g

Grill Cheese Sandwich

Servings:2
Cooking Time:10
Ingredients:

- 4 slices of white bread slices
- 2 tablespoons of butter, melted
- 2 slices of sharp cheddar
- 2 slices of Swiss cheese
- 2 slices of mozzarella cheese

Directions:

1. Brush melted butter on one side of all the bread slices and then top the 2 bread slices with slices of cheddar, Swiss, and mozzarella, one slice per bread.
2. Top it with the other slice to make a sandwich.
3. Divide it between two baskets of the air fryer.
4. Turn on AIR FRY mode for zone 1 basket at 350 degrees F for 10 minutes.
5. Use the MATCH button for the second zone.
6. Once done, serve.

Nutrition:

- (Per serving) Calories 577 | Fat38g | Sodium 1466mg | Carbs 30.5g | Fiber 1.1g| Sugar 6.5g | Protein 27.6g

Shrimp Pirogues

Servings: 8
Cooking Time: 4 To 5 Minutes
Ingredients:
- 340 g small, peeled, and deveined raw shrimp
- 85 g soft white cheese, room temperature
- 2 tablespoons natural yoghurt
- 1 teaspoon lemon juice
- 1 teaspoon dried dill weed, crushed
- Salt, to taste
- 4 small hothouse cucumbers, each approximately 6 inches long

Directions:
1. Pour 4 tablespoons water in bottom of air fryer drawer.
2. Place shrimp in air fryer basket in single layer and air fry at 200°C for 4 to 5 minutes, just until done. Watch carefully because shrimp cooks quickly, and overcooking makes it tough.
3. Chop shrimp into small pieces, no larger than ½ inch. Refrigerate while mixing the remaining ingredients.
4. With a fork, mash and whip the soft white cheese until smooth.
5. Stir in the yoghurt and beat until smooth. Stir in lemon juice, dill weed, and chopped shrimp.
6. Taste for seasoning. If needed, add ¼ to ½ teaspoon salt to suit your taste.
7. Store in refrigerator until serving time.
8. When ready to serve, wash and dry cucumbers and split them lengthwise. Scoop out the seeds and turn cucumbers upside down on paper towels to drain for 10 minutes.
9. Just before filling, wipe centres of cucumbers dry. Spoon the shrimp mixture into the pirogues and cut in half crosswise. Serve immediately.

Kale Chips

Servings: 4
Cooking Time: 3 Minutes
Ingredients:
- 1 head fresh kale, stems and ribs removed and cut into 4cm pieces
- 1 tablespoon olive oil
- 1 teaspoon soy sauce
- ⅛ teaspoon cayenne pepper
- Pinch of freshly ground black pepper

Directions:
1. In a large bowl, add all the ingredients and mix well.
2. Grease basket of Tefal 2-Basket Air Fryer.
3. Press your chosen zone - "Zone 1" or "Zone 2" and then rotate the knob to select "Air Fry".
4. Set the temperature to 200 degrees C and then set the time for 5 minutes to preheat.
5. After preheating, arrange the kale pieces into the basket of each zone.
6. Slide the basket into the Air Fryer and set the time for 3 minutes.
7. While cooking, toss the kale pieces once halfway through.
8. After cooking time is completed, remove the kale chips and baking pans from Air Fryer.
9. Place the kale chips onto a wire rack to cool for about 10 minutes before serving.

Crispy Plantain Chips

Servings: 4
Cooking Time: 20 Minutes.
Ingredients:
- 1 green plantain
- 1 teaspoon canola oil
- ½ teaspoon sea salt

Directions:
1. Peel and cut the plantains into long strips using a mandolin slicer.
2. Grease the crisper plates with ½ teaspoon of canola oil.
3. Toss the plantains with salt and remaining canola oil.
4. Divide these plantains in the two crisper plates.
5. Return the crisper plate to the Tefal Dual Zone Air Fryer.
6. Choose the Air Fry mode for Zone 1 and set the temperature to 350 degrees F and the time to 20 minutes.
7. Select the "MATCH" button to copy the settings for Zone 2.
8. Initiate cooking by pressing the START/STOP button.
9. Toss the plantains after 10 minutes and resume cooking.
10. Serve warm.

Nutrition:
- (Per serving) Calories 122 | Fat 1.8g |Sodium 794mg | Carbs 17g | Fiber 8.9g | Sugar 1.6g | Protein 14.9g

Crab Cake Poppers

Servings: 6
Cooking Time: 15 Minutes
Ingredients:

- 1 egg, lightly beaten
- 453g lump crab meat, drained
- 1 tsp garlic, minced
- 1 tsp lemon juice
- 1 tsp old bay seasoning
- 30g almond flour
- 1 tsp Dijon mustard
- 28g mayonnaise
- Pepper
- Salt

Directions:

1. In a bowl, mix crab meat and remaining ingredients until well combined.
2. Make small balls from the crab meat mixture and place them on a plate.
3. Place the plate in the refrigerator for 50 minutes.
4. Insert a crisper plate in the Tefal air fryer baskets.
5. Place the prepared crab meatballs in both baskets.
6. Select zone 1 then select "air fry" mode and set the temperature to 360 degrees F for 10 minutes. Press "match" to match zone 2 settings to zone 1. Press "start/stop" to begin.

Vegetables And Sides Recipes

Garlic Herbed Baked Potatoes

Servings: 4
Cooking Time: 45 Minutes
Ingredients:

- 4 large baking potatoes
- Salt and black pepper, to taste
- 2 teaspoons avocado oil
- Cheese
- 2 cups sour cream
- 1 teaspoon garlic clove, minced
- 1 teaspoon fresh dill
- 2 teaspoons chopped chives
- Salt and black pepper, to taste
- 2 teaspoons Worcestershire sauce

Directions:

1. Pierce the skin of the potatoes with a fork.
2. Season the potatoes with olive oil, salt, and black pepper.
3. Divide the potatoes into the air fryer baskets.
4. Now press 1 for zone 1 and set it to AIR FRY mode at 350 degrees F/ 175 degrees C, for 45 minutes.
5. Select the MATCH button for zone 2.
6. Meanwhile, take a bowl and mix all the cheese ingredients together.
7. Once the cooking cycle is complete, take out the potatoes and make a slit in-between each one.
8. Add the cheese mixture in the cavity and serve it hot.

Potatoes & Beans

Servings: 4
Cooking Time: 25 Minutes
Ingredients:

- 453g potatoes, cut into pieces
- 15ml olive oil
- 1 tsp garlic powder
- 160g green beans, trimmed
- Pepper
- Salt

Directions:

1. In a bowl, toss green beans, garlic powder, potatoes, oil, pepper, and salt.
2. Insert a crisper plate in the Tefal air fryer baskets.
3. Add green beans and potato mixture to both baskets.
4. Select zone 1 then select "air fry" mode and set the temperature to 380 degrees F for 25 minutes. Press "match" to match zone 2 settings to zone 1. Press "start/stop" to begin. Stir halfway through.

Nutrition:

- (Per serving) Calories 128 | Fat 3.7g |Sodium 49mg | Carbs 22.4g | Fiber 4.7g | Sugar 2.3g | Protein 3.1g

Fried Patty Pan Squash

Servings: 6
Cooking Time: 15 Minutes
Ingredients:
- 5 cups small pattypan squash, halved
- 1 tablespoon olive oil
- 2 garlic cloves, minced
- ½ teaspoon salt
- ¼ teaspoon dried oregano
- ¼ teaspoon dried thyme
- ¼ teaspoon pepper
- 1 tablespoon minced parsley

Directions:
1. Rub the squash with oil, garlic and the rest of the ingredients.
2. Spread the squash in the air fryer baskets.
3. Return the air fryer basket 1 to Zone 1, and basket 2 to Zone 2 of the Tefal 2-Basket Air Fryer.
4. Choose the "Air Fry" mode for Zone 1 at 375 degrees F and 15 minutes of cooking time.
5. Select the "MATCH COOK" option to copy the settings for Zone 2.
6. Initiate cooking by pressing the START/PAUSE BUTTON.
7. Flip the squash once cooked halfway through.
8. Garnish with parsley.
9. Serve warm.

Nutrition:
- (Per serving) Calories 208 | Fat 5g |Sodium 1205mg | Carbs 34.1g | Fiber 7.8g | Sugar 2.5g | Protein 5.9g

Mushroom Roll-ups

Servings: 10
Cooking Time: 10 Minutes
Ingredients:
- 2 tablespoons extra virgin olive oil
- 8 ounces large portobello mushrooms (gills discarded), finely chopped
- 1 teaspoon dried oregano
- 1 teaspoon dried thyme
- ½ teaspoon crushed red pepper flakes
- ¼ teaspoon salt
- 8 ounces cream cheese, softened
- 4 ounces whole-milk ricotta cheese
- 10 flour tortillas (8-inch)
- Cooking spray
- Chutney, for serving (optional)

Directions:
1. Heat the oil in a pan over medium heat. Add the mushrooms and cook for 4 minutes. Sauté until the mushrooms are browned, about 4-6 minutes, with the oregano, thyme, pepper flakes, and salt. Cool.
2. Combine the cheeses in a mixing bowl| fold in the mushrooms until thoroughly combined.
3. On the bottom center of each tortilla, spread 3 tablespoons of the mushroom mixture. Tightly roll up each tortilla and secure with toothpicks.
4. Place a crisper plate in each drawer. Put the roll-ups in a single layer in each. Insert the drawers into the unit.
5. Select zone 1, then AIR FRY, then set the temperature to 400 degrees F/ 200 degrees C with a 10-minute timer. To match zone 2 settings to zone 1, choose MATCH. To begin, select START/STOP.
6. Remove the roll-ups from the drawers after the timer has finished. When they have cooled enough to handle, discard the toothpicks.
7. Serve and enjoy!

Healthy Air Fried Veggies

Servings: 4
Cooking Time: 15 Minutes
Ingredients:
- 52g onion, sliced
- 71g broccoli florets
- 116g radishes, sliced
- 15ml olive oil
- 100g Brussels sprouts, cut in half
- 325g cauliflower florets
- 1 tsp balsamic vinegar
- ½ tsp garlic powder
- Pepper
- Salt

Directions:
1. In a bowl, toss veggies with oil, vinegar, garlic powder, pepper, and salt.
2. Insert a crisper plate in the Tefal air fryer baskets.
3. Add veggies in both baskets.
4. Select zone 1 then select "air fry" mode and set the temperature to 380 degrees F for 15 minutes. Press "match" to match zone 2 settings to zone 1. Press "start/stop" to begin. Stir halfway through.

Nutrition:
- (Per serving) Calories 71 | Fat 3.8g |Sodium 72mg | Carbs 8.8g | Fiber 3.2g | Sugar 3.3g | Protein 2.5g

Potato And Parsnip Latkes With Baked Apples

Servings:4

Cooking Time: 20 Minutes

Ingredients:

- FOR THE LATKES
- 2 medium russet potatoes, peeled
- 1 large egg white
- 2 tablespoons all-purpose flour
- ¼ teaspoon garlic powder
- ¼ teaspoon kosher salt
- ¼ teaspoon freshly ground black pepper
- 1 medium parsnip, peeled and shredded
- 2 scallions, thinly sliced
- 2 tablespoons vegetable oil
- FOR THE BAKED APPLES
- 2 Golden Delicious apples, peeled and diced
- 2 tablespoons granulated sugar
- 2 teaspoons unsalted butter, cut into small pieces

Directions:

1. To prep the latkes: Grate the potatoes using the large holes of a box grater. Squeeze as much liquid out of the potatoes as you can into a large bowl. Set the potatoes aside in a separate bowl.

2. Let the potato liquid sit for 5 minutes, during which time the potato starch will settle to the bottom of the bowl. Pour off the water that has risen to the top, leaving the potato starch in the bowl.

3. Add the egg white, flour, salt, and black pepper to the potato starch to form a thick paste. Add the potatoes, parsnip, and scallions and mix well. Divide the mixture into 4 patties. Brush both sides of each patty with the oil.

4. To prep the baked apples: Place the apples in the Zone 2 basket. Sprinkle the sugar and butter over the top.

5. To cook the latkes and apples: Install a crisper plate in the Zone 1 basket. Place the latkes in the basket in a single layer, then insert the basket in the unit. Insert the Zone 2 basket in the unit.

6. Select Zone 1, select AIR FRY, set the temperature to 375°F, and set the timer to 15 minutes.

7. Select Zone 2, select BAKE, set the temperature to 330°F, and set the timer to 20 minutes. Select SMART FINISH.

8. Press START/PAUSE to begin cooking.

9. When both timers read 5 minutes, press START/PAUSE. Remove the Zone 1 basket and use silicone-tipped tongs or a spatula to flip the latkes. Reinsert the basket in the unit. Remove the Zone 2 basket and gently mash the apples with a fork or the back of a spoon. Reinsert the basket and press START/PAUSE to resume cooking.

10. When cooking is complete, the latkes should be golden brown and cooked through and the apples very soft.

11. Transfer the latkes to a plate and serve with apples on the side.

Nutrition:

- (Per serving) Calories: 257; Total fat: 9g; Saturated fat: 2g; Carbohydrates: 42g; Fiber: 5.5g; Protein: 4g; Sodium: 91mg

Air Fryer Vegetables

Servings: 2

Cooking Time: 15 Minutes

Ingredients:

- 1 courgette, diced
- 2 capsicums, diced
- 1 head broccoli, diced
- 1 red onion, diced
- Marinade
- 1 teaspoon smoked paprika
- 1 teaspoon garlic granules
- 1 teaspoon Herb de Provence
- Salt and black pepper, to taste
- 1½ tablespoon olive oil
- 2 tablespoons lemon juice

Directions:

1. Toss the veggies with the rest of the marinade ingredients in a bowl.

2. Spread the veggies in the air fryer baskets.

3. Return the air fryer basket 1 to Zone 1, and basket 2 to Zone 2 of the Tefal 2-Basket Air Fryer.

4. Choose the "Air Fry" mode for Zone 1 at 400 degrees F and 15 minutes of cooking time.

5. Select the "MATCH COOK" option to copy the settings for Zone 2.

6. Initiate cooking by pressing the START/PAUSE BUTTON.

7. Toss the veggies once cooked half way through.

8. Serve warm.

Nutrition:

- (Per serving) Calories 166 | Fat 3.2g |Sodium 437mg | Carbs 28.8g | Fiber 1.8g | Sugar 2.7g | Protein 5.8g

Buffalo Bites

Servings: 6
Cooking Time: 30 Minutes
Ingredients:
- For the bites:
- 1 small cauliflower head, cut into florets
- 2 tablespoons olive oil
- 3 tablespoons buffalo wing sauce
- 3 tablespoons butter, melted
- For the dip:
- 1½ cups 2% cottage cheese
- ¼ cup fat-free plain Greek yogurt
- ¼ cup crumbled blue cheese
- 1 sachet ranch salad dressing mix
- Celery sticks (optional)

Directions:
1. In a large bowl, combine the cauliflower and oil| toss to coat.
2. Place a crisper plate in each drawer. Put the coated cauliflower florets in each drawer in a single layer. Place the drawers in the unit.
3. Select zone 1, then AIR FRY, then set the temperature to 360 degrees F/ 180 degrees C with a 15-minute timer. To match zone 2 settings to zone 1, choose MATCH. To begin, select START/STOP.
4. Remove the cauliflower from the drawers after the timer has finished.
5. Combine the buffalo sauce and melted butter in a large mixing bowl. Put in the cauliflower and toss to coat. Place on a serving dish and serve.
6. Combine the dip ingredients in a small bowl. Serve with the cauliflower and celery sticks, if desired.

Green Salad With Crispy Fried Goat Cheese And Baked Croutons

Servings:4
Cooking Time: 10 Minutes
Ingredients:
- FOR THE GOAT CHEESE
- 1 (4-ounce) log soft goat cheese
- ½ cup panko bread crumbs
- 2 tablespoons vegetable oil
- FOR THE CROUTONS
- 2 slices Italian-style sandwich bread
- 2 tablespoons vegetable oil
- 1 tablespoon poultry seasoning
- ½ teaspoon kosher salt
- ¼ teaspoon freshly ground black pepper
- FOR THE SALAD
- 8 cups green leaf lettuce leaves
- ½ cup store-bought balsamic vinaigrette

Directions:
1. To prep the goat cheese: Cut the goat cheese into 8 round slices.
2. Spread the panko on a plate. Gently press the cheese into the panko to coat on both sides. Drizzle with the oil.
3. To prep the croutons: Cut the bread into cubes and place them in a large bowl. Add the oil, poultry seasoning, salt, and black pepper. Mix well to coat the bread cubes evenly.
4. To cook the goat cheese and croutons: Install a crisper plate in each of the two baskets. Place the goat cheese in the Zone 1 basket and insert the basket in the unit. Place the croutons in the Zone 2 basket and insert the basket in the unit.
5. Select Zone 1, select AIR FRY, set the temperature to 400°F, and set the timer to 6 minutes.
6. Select Zone 2, select BAKE, set the temperature to 390°F, and set the timer to 10 minutes. Select SMART FINISH.
7. Press START/PAUSE to begin cooking.
8. When cooking is complete, the goat cheese will be golden brown and the croutons crisp.
9. Remove the Zone 1 basket. Let the goat cheese cool in the basket for 5 minutes; it will firm up as it cools.
10. To assemble the salad: In a large bowl, combine the lettuce, vinaigrette, and croutons. Toss well. Divide the salad among four plates. Top each plate with 2 pieces of goat cheese.

Nutrition:
- (Per serving) Calories: 578; Total fat: 40g; Saturated fat: 14g; Carbohydrates: 39g; Fiber: 3.5g; Protein: 24g; Sodium: 815mg

Spanakopita Rolls With Mediterranean Vegetable Salad

Servings:4
Cooking Time: 15 Minutes
Ingredients:

- FOR THE SPANAKOPITA ROLLS
- 1 (10-ounce) package chopped frozen spinach, thawed
- 4 ounces feta cheese, crumbled
- 2 large eggs
- 1 teaspoon dried oregano
- ½ teaspoon freshly ground black pepper
- 12 sheets phyllo dough, thawed
- Nonstick cooking spray
- FOR THE ROASTED VEGETABLES
- 1 medium eggplant, diced
- 1 small red onion, cut into 8 wedges
- 1 red bell pepper, sliced
- 2 tablespoons olive oil
- FOR THE SALAD
- 1 (15-ounce) can chickpeas, drained and rinsed
- ¼ cup chopped fresh parsley
- ¼ cup olive oil
- ¼ cup red wine vinegar
- 2 garlic cloves, minced
- ½ teaspoon dried oregano
- ¼ teaspoon kosher salt
- ¼ teaspoon freshly ground black pepper

Directions:

1. To prep the spanakopita rolls: Squeeze as much liquid from the spinach as you can and place the spinach in a large bowl. Add the feta, eggs, oregano, and black pepper. Mix well.
2. Lay one sheet of phyllo on a clean work surface and mist it with cooking spray. Place another sheet of phyllo directly on top of the first sheet and mist it with cooking spray. Repeat with a third sheet.
3. Spoon one-quarter of the spinach mixture along one short side of the phyllo. Fold the long sides in over the spinach, then roll up it like a burrito.
4. Repeat this process with the remaining phyllo sheets and spinach mixture to form 4 rolls.
5. To prep the vegetables: In a large bowl, combine the eggplant, onion, bell pepper, and oil. Mix well.
6. To cook the rolls and vegetables: Install a crisper plate in each of the two baskets. Place the spanakopita rolls seam-side down in the Zone 1 basket, and spritz the rolls with cooking spray. Place the vegetables in the Zone 2 basket and insert both baskets in the unit.
7. Select Zone 1, select AIR FRY, set the temperature to 375°F, and set the timer to 10 minutes.
8. Select Zone 2, select ROAST, set the temperature to 375°F, and set the timer to 15 minutes. Select SMART FINISH.
9. Press START/PAUSE to begin cooking.
10. When the Zone 1 timer reads 3 minutes, press START/PAUSE. Remove the basket and use silicone-tipped tongs or a spatula to flip the spanakopita rolls. Reinsert the basket and press START/PAUSE to resume cooking.
11. When cooking is complete, the rolls should be crisp and golden brown and the vegetables tender.
12. To assemble the salad: Transfer the roasted vegetables to a large bowl. Stir in the chickpeas and parsley.
13. In a small bowl, whisk together the oil, vinegar, garlic, oregano, salt, and black pepper. Pour the dressing over the vegetables and toss to coat. Serve warm.

Nutrition:

- (Per serving) Calories: 739; Total fat: 51g; Saturated fat: 8g; Carbohydrates: 67g; Fiber: 11g; Protein: 21g; Sodium: 806mg

Garlic-herb Fried Squash

Servings: 4
Cooking Time: 15 Minutes
Ingredients:

- 5 cups halved small pattypan squash (about 1¼ pounds)
- 1 tablespoon olive oil
- 2 garlic cloves, minced
- ½ teaspoon salt
- ¼ teaspoon dried oregano
- ¼ teaspoon dried thyme
- ¼ teaspoon pepper
- 1 tablespoon minced fresh parsley, for serving

Directions:

1. Place the squash in a large bowl.
2. Mix the oil, garlic, salt, oregano, thyme, and pepper| drizzle over the squash. Toss to coat.
3. Place a crisper plate in both drawers. Put the squash in a single layer in each drawer. Insert the drawers into the unit.
4. Select zone 1, then AIR FRY, then set the temperature to 360 degrees F/ 180 degrees C with a 6-minute timer. To match zone 2 settings to zone 1, choose MATCH. To begin, select START/STOP.
5. Remove the squash from the drawers after the timer has finished. Sprinkle with the parsley.

Fresh Mix Veggies In Air Fryer

Servings: 4
Cooking Time: 12 Minutes
Ingredients:

- 1 cup cauliflower florets
- 1 cup carrots, peeled chopped
- 1 cup broccoli florets
- 2 tablespoons avocado oil
- Salt, to taste
- ½ teaspoon chili powder
- ½ teaspoon garlic powder
- ½ teaspoon herbs de Provence
- 1 cup Parmesan cheese

Directions:

1. Take a bowl, and add all the veggies to it.
2. Toss and then season the veggies with salt, chili powder, garlic powder, and herbs de Provence.
3. Toss it all well and then drizzle avocado oil.
4. Make sure the ingredients are coated well.
5. Distribute the veggies among both baskets of the air fryer.
6. Turn on the START/STOP button and set it to AIR FRY mode at 390 degrees F/ 200 degrees C for 10-12 minutes.
7. For the zone 2 basket setting, press the MATCH button.
8. After 8 minutes of cooking, press the START/STOP button and then take out the baskets and sprinkle Parmesan cheese on top of the veggies.
9. Then let the cooking cycle complete for the next 3-4 minutes.
10. Once done, serve.

Zucchini Cakes

Servings: 6
Cooking Time: 32 Minutes
Ingredients:

- 2 medium zucchinis, grated
- 1 cup corn kernel
- 1 medium potato cooked
- 2 tablespoons chickpea flour
- 2 garlic minced
- 2 teaspoons olive oil
- Salt and black pepper
- For Serving:
- Yogurt tahini sauce

Directions:

1. Mix grated zucchini with a pinch of salt in a colander and leave them for 15 minutes.
2. Squeeze out their excess water.

3. Mash the cooked potato in a large-sized bowl with a fork.
4. Add zucchini, corn, garlic, chickpea flour, salt, and black pepper to the bowl. 5. Mix these fritters' ingredients together and make 2 tablespoons-sized balls out of this mixture and flatten them lightly.
5. Divide the fritters in the two crisper plates in a single layer and spray them with cooking.
6. Return the crisper plates to the Tefal Dual Zone Air Fryer.
7. Choose the Air Fry mode for Zone 1 and set the temperature to 390 degrees F/ 200 degrees C and the time to 17 minutes.
8. Select the "MATCH" button to copy the settings for Zone 2.
9. Initiate cooking by pressing the START/STOP button.
10. Flip the fritters once cooked halfway through, then resume cooking.
11. Serve.

Bacon Potato Patties

Servings: 2
Cooking Time: 15 Minutes
Ingredients:

- 1 egg
- 600g mashed potatoes
- 119g breadcrumbs
- 2 bacon slices, cooked & chopped
- 235g cheddar cheese, shredded
- 15g flour
- Pepper
- Salt

Directions:

1. In a bowl, mix mashed potatoes with remaining ingredients until well combined.
2. Make patties from potato mixture and place on a plate.
3. Place plate in the refrigerator for 10 minutes
4. Insert a crisper plate in the Tefal air fryer baskets.
5. Place the prepared patties in both baskets.
6. Select zone 1 then select "air fry" mode and set the temperature to 390 degrees F for 15 minutes. Press "match" to match zone 2 settings to zone 1. Press "start/stop" to begin. Turn halfway through.

Nutrition:

- (Per serving) Calories 702 | Fat 26.8g |Sodium 1405mg | Carbs 84.8g | Fiber 2.7g | Sugar 3.8g | Protein 30.5g

Air-fried Tofu Cutlets With Cacio E Pepe Brussels Sprouts

Servings:4

Cooking Time: 25 Minutes

Ingredients:

- FOR THE TOFU CUTLETS
- 1 (14-ounce) package extra-firm tofu, drained
- 1 cup panko bread crumbs
- ¼ cup grated pecorino romano or Parmesan cheese
- 1 teaspoon garlic powder
- 1 teaspoon onion powder
- ¼ teaspoon kosher salt
- 1 tablespoon vegetable oil
- 4 lemon wedges, for serving
- FOR THE BRUSSELS SPROUTS
- 1 pound Brussels sprouts, trimmed
- 1 tablespoon vegetable oil
- 2 tablespoons grated pecorino romano or Parmesan cheese
- ½ teaspoon freshly ground black pepper, plus more to taste
- ¼ teaspoon kosher salt

Directions:

1. To prep the tofu: Cut the tofu horizontally into 4 slabs.

2. In a shallow bowl, mix together the panko, cheese, garlic powder, onion powder, and salt. Press both sides of each tofu slab into the panko mixture. Drizzle both sides with the oil.

3. To prep the Brussels sprouts: Cut the Brussels sprouts in half through the root end.

4. In a large bowl, combine the Brussels sprouts and olive oil. Mix to coat.

5. To cook the tofu cutlets and Brussels sprouts: Install a crisper plate in each of the two baskets. Place the tofu cutlets in a single layer in the Zone 1 basket and insert the basket in the unit. Place the Brussels sprouts in the Zone 2 basket and insert the basket in the unit.

6. Select Zone 1, select AIR FRY, set the temperature to 400°F, and set the timer to 20 minutes.

7. Select Zone 2, select ROAST, set the temperature to 400°F, and set the timer to 25 minutes. Select SMART FINISH.

8. Press START/PAUSE to begin cooking.

9. When both timers read 5 minutes, press START/PAUSE. Remove the Zone 1 basket and use a pair of silicone-tipped tongs to flip the tofu cutlets, then reinsert the basket in the unit. Remove the Zone 2 basket and sprinkle the cheese and black pepper over the Brussels sprouts. Reinsert the basket and press START/PAUSE to resume cooking.

10. When cooking is complete, the tofu should be crisp and the Brussels sprouts tender and beginning to brown.

11. Squeeze the lemon wedges over the tofu cutlets. Stir the Brussels sprouts, then season with the salt and additional black pepper to taste.

Nutrition:

- (Per serving) Calories: 319; Total fat: 15g; Saturated fat: 3.5g; Carbohydrates: 27g; Fiber: 6g; Protein: 20g; Sodium: 402mg

Bacon Wrapped Corn Cob

Servings: 4

Cooking Time: 10 Minutes

Ingredients:

- 4 trimmed corns on the cob
- 8 bacon slices

Directions:

1. Wrap the corn cobs with two bacon slices.

2. Place the wrapped cobs into the Tefal 2 Baskets Air Fryer baskets.

3. Return the air fryer basket 1 to Zone 1, and basket 2 to Zone 2 of the Tefal 2-Basket Air Fryer.

4. Choose the "Air Fry" mode for Zone 1 and set the temperature to 355 degrees F and 10 minutes of cooking time.

5. Select the "MATCH COOK" option to copy the settings for Zone 2.

6. Initiate cooking by pressing the START/PAUSE BUTTON.

7. Flip the corn cob once cooked halfway through.

8. Serve warm.

Nutrition:

- (Per serving) Calories 350 | Fat 2.6g |Sodium 358mg | Carbs 64.6g | Fiber 14.4g | Sugar 3.3g | Protein 19.9g

Garlic-rosemary Brussels Sprouts

Servings: 4
Cooking Time: 15 Minutes
Ingredients:

- 3 tablespoons olive oil
- 2 garlic cloves, minced
- ½ teaspoon salt
- ¼ teaspoon pepper
- 1-pound Brussels sprouts, trimmed and halved
- ½ cup panko breadcrumbs
- 1½ teaspoons minced fresh rosemary

Directions:

1. Place the first 4 ingredients in a small microwave-safe bowl| microwave on high for 30 seconds.
2. Toss the Brussels sprouts in 2 tablespoons of the microwaved mixture.
3. Place a crisper plate in each drawer. Put the sprouts in a single layer in each drawer. Insert the drawers into the units.
4. Select zone 1, then AIR FRY, then set the temperature to 360 degrees F/ 180 degrees C with a 6-minute timer. To match zone 2 settings to zone 1, choose MATCH. To begin, select START/STOP.
5. Remove the sprouts from the drawers after the timer has finished.
6. Toss the breadcrumbs with the rosemary and remaining oil mixture| sprinkle over the sprouts.
7. Continue cooking until the crumbs are browned, and the sprouts are tender . Serve immediately.

Zucchini With Stuffing

Servings:3
Cooking Time:20
Ingredients:

- 1 cup quinoa, rinsed
- 1 cup black olives
- 6 medium zucchinis, about 2 pounds
- 2 cups cannellini beans, drained
- 1 white onion, chopped
- ¼ cup almonds, chopped
- 4 cloves of garlic, chopped
- 4 tablespoons olive oil
- 1 cup of water
- 2 cups Parmesan cheese, for topping

Directions:

1. First wash the zucchini and cut it lengthwise.
2. Take a skillet and heat oil in it

3. Sauté the onion in olive oil for a few minutes.
4. Then add the quinoa and water and let it cook for 8 minutes with the lid on the top.
5. Transfer the quinoa to a bowl and add all remaining ingredients excluding zucchini and Parmesan cheese.
6. Scoop out the seeds of zucchinis.
7. Fill the cavity of zucchinis with bowl mixture.
8. Top it with a handful of Parmesan cheese.
9. Arrange 4 zucchinis in both air fryer baskets.
10. Select zone1 basket at AIR FRY for 20 minutes and adjusting the temperature to 390 degrees F.
11. Use the Match button to select the same setting for zone 2.
12. Serve and enjoy.

Nutrition:

- (Per serving) Calories 1171| Fat 48.6g| Sodium 1747mg | Carbs 132.4g | Fiber 42.1g | Sugar 11.5g | Protein 65.7g

Garlic Potato Wedges In Air Fryer

Servings: 2
Cooking Time: 23 Minutes
Ingredients:

- 4 medium potatoes, peeled and cut into wedges
- 4 tablespoons butter
- 1 teaspoon chopped cilantro
- 1 cup plain flour
- 1 teaspoon garlic, minced
- Salt and black pepper, to taste

Directions:

1. Soak the potato wedges in cold water for about 30 minutes.
2. Drain and pat dry with a paper towel.
3. Boil water in a large pot and boil the wedges for 3 minutes and place on a paper towel.
4. In a bowl, mix garlic, melted butter, salt, pepper, and cilantro.
5. Add the flour to a separate bowl along with the salt and black pepper.
6. Add water to the flour so it gets a runny in texture.
7. Coat the potatoes with the flour mixture and divide them into two foil tins. 8. Place the foil tins in each air fryer basket.
8. Set the zone 1 basket to AIR FRY mode at 390 degrees F/ 200 degrees C for 20 minutes.
9. Select the MATCH button for the zone 2 basket. 11. Once done, serve and enjoy.

Delicious Potatoes & Carrots

Servings: 8
Cooking Time: 25 Minutes
Ingredients:

- 453g carrots, sliced
- 2 tsp smoked paprika
- 21g sugar
- 30ml olive oil
- 453g potatoes, diced
- ¼ tsp thyme
- ½ tsp dried oregano
- 1 tsp garlic powder
- Pepper
- Salt

Directions:

1. In a bowl, toss carrots and potatoes with 1 tablespoon of oil.
2. Insert a crisper plate in the Tefal air fryer baskets.
3. Add carrots and potatoes to both baskets.
4. Select zone 1 then select "air fry" mode and set the temperature to 390 degrees F for 15 minutes. Press "match" to match zone 2 settings to zone 1. Press "start/stop" to begin.
5. In a mixing bowl, add cooked potatoes, carrots, smoked paprika, sugar, oil, thyme, oregano, garlic powder, pepper, and salt and toss well.
6. Return carrot and potato mixture into the air fryer basket and cook for 10 minutes more.

Nutrition:

- (Per serving) Calories 101 | Fat 3.6g |Sodium 62mg | Carbs 16.6g | Fiber 3g | Sugar 5.1g | Protein 1.6g

Desserts Recipes

Honeyed, Roasted Apples With Walnuts & Rhubarb And Strawberry Crumble

Servings: 10
Cooking Time: 12 To 17 Minutes
Ingredients:

- Honeyed, Roasted Apples with Walnuts:
- 2 Granny Smith apples
- 20 g certified gluten-free rolled oats
- 2 tablespoons honey
- ½ teaspoon ground cinnamon
- 2 tablespoons chopped walnuts
- Pinch salt
- 1 tablespoon olive oil
- Rhubarb and Strawberry Crumble:
- 250 g sliced fresh strawberries
- 95 g sliced rhubarb
- 75 g granulated sugar
- 60 g quick-cooking oatmeal
- 50 g whole-wheat pastry flour, or plain flour
- 50 g packed light brown sugar
- ½ teaspoon ground cinnamon
- 3 tablespoons unsalted butter, melted

Directions:

1. Make the Honeyed, Roasted Apples with Walnuts :
2. Preheat the air fryer to 190ºC.
3. Core the apples and slice them in half.
4. In a medium bowl, mix together the oats, honey, cinnamon, walnuts, salt, and olive oil.
5. Scoop a quarter of the oat mixture onto the top of each half apple.
6. Place the apples in the zone 1 air fryer basket, and roast for 12 to 15 minutes, or until the apples are fork tender.
7. Make the Rhubarb and Strawberry Crumble :
8. Preheat the air fryer to 190ºC.
9. In a 6-by-2-inch round metal baking pan, combine the strawberries, rhubarb, and granulated sugar.
10. In a medium bowl, stir together the oatmeal, flour, brown sugar, and cinnamon. Stir the melted butter into this mixture until crumbly. Sprinkle the crumble mixture over the fruit.
11. Once the unit is preheated, place the pan into the zone 2 basket.
12. Bake for 12 minutes then check the crumble. If the fruit is bubbling and the topping is golden brown, it is done. If not, resume cooking.
13. When the cooking is complete, serve warm.

Lemony Sweet Twists

Servings: 2
Cooking Time: 10 Minutes
Ingredients:
- 1 box store-bought puff pastry
- ½ teaspoon lemon zest
- 1 tablespoon lemon juice
- 2 teaspoons brown sugar
- Salt, pinch
- 2 tablespoons Parmesan cheese, freshly grated

Directions:
1. Put the puff pastry dough on a clean work surface.
2. In a bowl, combine Parmesan cheese, brown sugar, salt, lemon zest, and lemon juice.
3. Press this mixture into both sides of the dough.
4. Now, cut the pastry into 1" x 4" strips.
5. Twist 2 times from each end.
6. Place the strips into the air fryer baskets.
7. Select zone 1 to AIR FRY mode at 400 degrees F for 9-10 minutes.
8. Select MATCH for zone 2 basket.
9. Once cooked, serve and enjoy.

Gluten-free Spice Cookies

Servings: 4
Cooking Time: 12 Minutes
Ingredients:
- 4 tablespoons unsalted butter, at room temperature
- 2 tablespoons agave nectar
- 1 large egg
- 2 tablespoons water
- 240 g almond flour
- 100 g granulated sugar
- 2 teaspoons ground ginger
- 1 teaspoon ground cinnamon
- ½ teaspoon freshly grated nutmeg
- 1 teaspoon baking soda
- ¼ teaspoon kosher, or coarse sea salt

Directions:
1. Line the bottom of the air fryer basket with baking paper cut to fit.
2. In a large bowl, using a hand mixer, beat together the butter, agave, egg, and water on medium speed until light and fluffy.
3. Add the almond flour, sugar, ginger, cinnamon, nutmeg, baking soda, and salt. Beat on low speed until well combined.

4. Roll the dough into 2-tablespoon balls and arrange them on the baking paper in the basket. Set the air fryer to 165°C, and cook for 12 minutes, or until the tops of cookies are lightly browned.
5. Transfer to a wire rack and let cool completely. Store in an airtight container for up to a week.

Lemon Raspberry Muffins

Servings: 6
Cooking Time: 15 Minutes
Ingredients:
- 220 g almond flour
- 75 g powdered sweetener
- 1¼ teaspoons baking powder
- ⅓ teaspoon ground allspice
- ⅓ teaspoon ground star anise
- ½ teaspoon grated lemon zest
- ¼ teaspoon salt
- 2 eggs
- 240 ml sour cream
- 120 ml coconut oil
- 60 g raspberries

Directions:
1. Preheat the air fryer to 176°C. Line a muffin pan with 6 paper cases.
2. In a mixing bowl, mix the almond flour, sweetener, baking powder, allspice, star anise, lemon zest, and salt.
3. In another mixing bowl, beat the eggs, sour cream, and coconut oil until well mixed. Add the egg mixture to the flour mixture and stir to combine. Mix in the raspberries.
4. Scrape the batter into the prepared muffin cups, filling each about three-quarters full.
5. Bake for 15 minutes, or until the tops are golden and a toothpick inserted in the middle comes out clean.
6. Allow the muffins to cool for 10 minutes in the muffin pan before removing and serving.

Mocha Pudding Cake Vanilla Pudding Cake

Servings: 8
Cooking Time: 25 Minutes
Ingredients:
- FOR THE MOCHA PUDDING CAKE
- 1 cup all-purpose flour
- ⅔ cup granulated sugar
- 1 cup packed light brown sugar, divided
- 5 tablespoons unsweetened cocoa powder, divided
- 2 teaspoons baking powder
- ¼ teaspoon kosher salt
- ½ cup unsweetened almond milk
- 2 teaspoons vanilla extract
- 2 tablespoons vegetable oil
- 1 cup freshly brewed coffee
- FOR THE VANILLA PUDDING CAKE
- 1 cup all-purpose flour
- ⅔ cup granulated sugar, plus ½ cup
- 2 teaspoons baking powder
- ¼ teaspoon kosher salt
- ½ cup unsweetened almond milk
- 2½ teaspoons vanilla extract, divided
- 2 tablespoons vegetable oil
- ¾ cup hot water
- 2 teaspoons cornstarch

Directions:
1. To prep the mocha pudding cake: In a medium bowl, combine the flour, granulated sugar, ½ cup of brown sugar, 3 tablespoons of cocoa powder, the baking powder, and salt. Stir in the almond milk, vanilla, and oil to form a thick batter.
2. Spread the batter in the bottom of the Zone 1 basket. Sprinkle the remaining ½ cup brown sugar and 2 tablespoons of cocoa powder in an even layer over the batter. Gently pour the hot coffee over the batter (do not mix).
3. To prep the vanilla pudding cake: In a medium bowl, combine the flour, ⅔ cup of granulated sugar, the baking powder, and salt. Stir in the almond milk, 2 teaspoons of vanilla, and the oil to form a thick batter.
4. Spread the batter in the bottom of the Zone 2 basket.
5. In a small bowl, whisk together the hot water, cornstarch, and remaining ½ cup of sugar and ½ teaspoon of vanilla. Gently pour over the batter (do not mix).

6. To cook both pudding cakes: Insert both baskets in the unit.
7. Select Zone 1, select BAKE, set the temperature to 330°F, and set the timer to 25 minutes. Select MATCH COOK to match Zone 2 settings to Zone 1.
8. Press START/PAUSE to begin cooking.
9. When cooking is complete, the tops of the cakes should be dry and set.
10. Let the cakes rest for 10 minutes before serving. The pudding will thicken as it cools.

Nutrition:
- (Per serving) Calories: 531; Total fat: 8g; Saturated fat: 1g; Carbohydrates: 115g; Fiber: 3.5g; Protein: 5g; Sodium: 111mg

Lime Bars

Servings: 12 Bars
Cooking Time: 33 Minutes
Ingredients:
- 140 g blanched finely ground almond flour, divided
- 75 g powdered sweetener, divided
- 4 tablespoons salted butter, melted
- 120 ml fresh lime juice
- 2 large eggs, whisked

Directions:
1. In a medium bowl, mix together 110 g flour, 25 g sweetener, and butter. Press mixture into bottom of an ungreased round nonstick cake pan.
2. Place pan into the zone 1 air fryer drawer. Adjust the temperature to 148°C and bake for 13 minutes. Crust will be brown and set in the middle when done.
3. Allow to cool in pan 10 minutes.
4. In a medium bowl, combine remaining flour, remaining sweetener, lime juice, and eggs. Pour mixture over cooled crust and return to air fryer for 20 minutes. Top will be browned and firm when done.
5. Let cool completely in pan, about 30 minutes, then chill covered in the refrigerator 1 hour. Serve chilled.

Crustless Peanut Butter Cheesecake And Pumpkin Pudding With Vanilla Wafers

Servings: 6
Cooking Time: 17 Minutes
Ingredients:

- Crustless Peanut Butter Cheesecake:
- 110 g cream cheese, softened
- 2 tablespoons powdered sweetener
- 1 tablespoon all-natural, no-sugar-added peanut butter
- ½ teaspoon vanilla extract
- 1 large egg, whisked
- Pumpkin Pudding with Vanilla Wafers:
- 250 g canned no-salt-added pumpkin purée (not pumpkin pie filling)
- 50 g packed brown sugar
- 3 tablespoons plain flour
- 1 egg, whisked
- 2 tablespoons milk
- 1 tablespoon unsalted butter, melted
- 1 teaspoon pure vanilla extract
- 4 low-fat vanilla, or plain wafers, crumbled
- Nonstick cooking spray

Directions:

1. Make the Crustless Peanut Butter Cheesecake :
2. In a medium bowl, mix cream cheese and sweetener until smooth. Add peanut butter and vanilla, mixing until smooth. Add egg and stir just until combined.
3. Spoon mixture into an ungreased springform pan and place into the zone 1 air fryer drawer. Adjust the temperature to 148°C and bake for 10 minutes. Edges will be firm, but center will be mostly set with only a small amount of jiggle when done.
4. Let pan cool at room temperature 30 minutes, cover with plastic wrap, then place into refrigerator at least 2 hours. Serve chilled.
5. Make the Pumpkin Pudding with Vanilla Wafers :
6. Preheat the air fryer to 176°C. Coat a baking pan with nonstick cooking spray. Set aside.
7. Mix the pumpkin purée, brown sugar, flour, whisked egg, milk, melted butter, and vanilla in a medium bowl and whisk to combine. Transfer the mixture to the baking pan.
8. Place the baking pan in the zone 2 air fryer drawer and bake for 12 to 17 minutes until set.
9. Remove the pudding from the drawer to a wire rack to cool.
10. Divide the pudding into four bowls and serve with the vanilla wafers sprinkled on top.

Moist Chocolate Espresso Muffins

Servings: 8
Cooking Time: 18 Minutes
Ingredients:

- 1 egg
- 177ml milk
- ½ tsp baking soda
- ½ tsp espresso powder
- ½ tsp baking powder
- 50g cocoa powder
- 78ml vegetable oil
- 1 tsp apple cider vinegar
- 1 tsp vanilla
- 150g brown sugar
- 150g all-purpose flour
- ½ tsp salt

Directions:

1. In a bowl, whisk egg, vinegar, oil, brown sugar, vanilla, and milk.
2. Add flour, cocoa powder, baking soda, baking powder, espresso powder, and salt and stir until well combined.
3. Pour batter into the silicone muffin moulds.
4. Insert a crisper plate in Tefal air fryer baskets.
5. Place muffin moulds in both baskets.
6. Select zone 1 then select "bake" mode and set the temperature to 320 degrees F for 18 minutes. Press match cook to match zone 2 settings to zone 1. Press "start/stop" to begin.

Nutrition:

- (Per serving) Calories 222 | Fat 11g |Sodium 251mg | Carbs 29.6g | Fiber 2g | Sugar 14.5g | Protein 4g

Soft Pecan Brownies

Servings: 6
Cooking Time: 20 Minutes
Ingredients:

- ½ cup blanched finely ground almond flour
- ½ cup powdered erythritol
- 2 tablespoons unsweetened cocoa powder
- ½ teaspoon baking powder
- ¼ cup unsalted butter, softened
- 1 large egg
- ¼ cup chopped pecans
- ¼ cup low-carb, sugar-free chocolate chips

Directions:

1. Stir erythritol, almond flour, baking powder and cocoa powder in a large bowl. Add in egg and butter, mix well.
2. Fold in chocolate chips and pecans. Pour mixture into 6&quot| round baking pan. Put pan into the air fryer basket.
3. Set the temperature to 300°F, then set the timer for 20 minutes.
4. A toothpick inserted in center will come out clean when completely cooked. Let it rest for 20 minutes to fully cool and firm up. Serve immediately.

Brownies Muffins

Servings: 3
Cooking Time: 10 Minutes
Ingredients:

- ¼ egg
- ⅛ cup walnuts, chopped
- 1 tablespoon vegetable oil
- ¼ package fudge brownie mix
- ½ teaspoon water

Directions:

1. Take a bowl, add all the ingredients. Mix well.
2. Place the mixture into prepared muffin molds evenly.
3. Line each basket of "Zone 1" and "Zone 2" with parchment paper.
4. Press "Zone 1" and "Zone 2" and then rotate the knob for each zone to select "Air Fry".
5. Set the temperature to 300 degrees F/ 150 degrees C for both zones and then set the time for 5 minutes to preheat.
6. After preheating, arrange the muffin molds into the basket of each zone.
7. Slide each basket into Air Fryer and set the time for 10 minutes.

8. After cooking time is completed, remove from Air Fryer.
9. Refrigerate.
10. Serve and enjoy!

Lava Cake

Servings: 4
Cooking Time: 15 Minutes
Ingredients:

- 1 cup semi-sweet chocolate chips
- 8 tablespoons butter
- 4 eggs
- 2 teaspoons vanilla extract
- ½ teaspoon salt
- 6 tablespoons all-purpose flour
- 1 cup powdered sugar
- For the chocolate filling:
- 2 tablespoons Nutella
- 1 tablespoon butter, softened
- 1 tablespoon powdered sugar

Directions:

1. Heat the chocolate chips and butter in a medium-sized microwave-safe bowl in 30-second intervals until thoroughly melted and smooth, stirring after each interval.
2. Whisk together the eggs, vanilla, salt, flour, and powdered sugar in a mixing bowl.
3. Combine the Nutella, softened butter, and powdered sugar in a separate bowl.
4. Spray 4 ramekins with oil and fill them halfway with the chocolate chip mixture. Fill each ramekin halfway with Nutella, then top with the remaining chocolate chip mixture, making sure the Nutella is well covered.
5. Install a crisper plate in both drawers. Place 2 ramekins in each drawer and insert the drawers into the unit.
6. Select zone 1, select AIR FRY, set temperature to 390°F, and set time to 22 minutes. Select MATCH to match zone 2 settings to zone 1. Press the START/STOP button to begin cooking.
7. Serve hot.

Banana Spring Rolls With Hot Fudge Dip

Servings:4
Cooking Time: 10 Minutes
Ingredients:
- FOR THE BANANA SPRING ROLLS
- 1 large banana
- 4 egg roll wrappers
- 4 teaspoons light brown sugar
- Nonstick cooking spray
- FOR THE HOT FUDGE DIP
- ¼ cup sweetened condensed milk
- 2 tablespoons semisweet chocolate chips
- 1 tablespoon unsweetened cocoa powder
- 1 tablespoon unsalted butter
- ⅛ teaspoon kosher salt
- ⅛ teaspoon vanilla extract

Directions:
1. To prep the banana spring rolls: Peel the banana and halve it crosswise. Cut each piece in half lengthwise, for a total of 4 pieces.
2. Place one piece of banana diagonally across an egg roll wrapper. Sprinkle with 1 teaspoon of brown sugar. Fold the edges of the egg roll wrapper over the ends of the banana, then roll to enclose the banana inside. Brush the edge of the wrapper with water and press to seal. Spritz with cooking spray. Repeat with the remaining bananas, egg roll wrappers, and brown sugar.
3. To prep the hot fudge dip: In an ovenproof ramekin or bowl, combine the condensed milk, chocolate chips, cocoa powder, butter, salt, and vanilla.
4. To cook the spring rolls and hot fudge dip: Install a crisper plate in each of the two baskets. Place the banana spring rolls seam-side down in the Zone 1 basket and insert the basket in the unit. Place the ramekin in the Zone 2 basket and insert the basket in the unit.
5. Select Zone 1, select AIR FRY, set the temperature to 390°F, and set the timer to 10 minutes.
6. Select Zone 2, select BAKE, set the temperature to 330°F, and set the timer to 8 minutes. Select SMART FINISH.
7. Press START/PAUSE to begin cooking.
8. When the Zone 2 timer reads 3 minutes, press START/PAUSE. Remove the basket and stir the hot fudge until smooth. Reinsert the basket and press START/PAUSE to resume cooking.
9. When cooking is complete, the spring rolls should be crisp.
10. Let the hot fudge cool for 2 to 3 minutes. Serve the banana spring rolls with hot fudge for dipping.
Nutrition:
- (Per serving) Calories: 268; Total fat: 10g; Saturated fat: 4g; Carbohydrates: 42g; Fiber: 2g; Protein: 5g; Sodium: 245mg

Blueberry Pie Egg Rolls

Servings: 12
Cooking Time: 5 Minutes
Ingredients:
- 12 egg roll wrappers
- 2 cups of blueberries
- 1 tablespoon of cornstarch
- ½ cup of agave nectar
- 1 teaspoon of lemon zest
- 2 tablespoons of water
- 1 tablespoon of lemon juice
- Olive oil or butter flavored cooking spray
- Confectioner's sugar for dusting

Directions:
1. Mix blueberries with cornstarch, lemon zest, agave and water in a saucepan.
2. Cook this mixture for 5 minutes on a simmer.
3. Allow the mixture to cool.
4. Spread the roll wrappers and divide the filling at the center of the wrappers.
5. Fold the two edges and roll each wrapper.
6. Wet and seal the wrappers then place them in the air fryer basket 1.
7. Spray these rolls with cooking spray.
8. Return the air fryer basket 1 to Zone 1 of the Tefal 2-Basket Air Fryer.
9. Choose the "Air Fry" mode for Zone 1 at 350 degrees F and 5 minutes of cooking time.
10. Initiate cooking by pressing the START/PAUSE BUTTON.
11. Dust the rolls with confectioner' sugar.
12. Serve.
Nutrition:
- (Per serving) Calories 258 | Fat 12.4g |Sodium 79mg | Carbs 34.3g | Fiber 1g | Sugar 17g | Protein 3.2g

Caramelized Fruit Skewers

Servings: 4
Cooking Time: 3 To 5 Minutes
Ingredients:

- 2 peaches, peeled, pitted, and thickly sliced
- 3 plums, halved and pitted
- 3 nectarines, halved and pitted
- 1 tablespoon honey
- ½ teaspoon ground cinnamon
- ¼ teaspoon ground allspice
- Pinch cayenne pepper
- Special Equipment:
- 8 metal skewers

Directions:

1. Preheat the air fryer to 204ºC.
2. Thread, alternating peaches, plums, and nectarines, onto the metal skewers that fit into the air fryer.
3. Thoroughly combine the honey, cinnamon, allspice, and cayenne in a small bowl. Brush the glaze generously over the fruit skewers.
4. Transfer the fruit skewers to the two air fryer drawers.
5. Air fry for 3 to 5 minutes, or until the fruit is caramelized.
6. Remove from the drawers.
7. Let the fruit skewers rest for 5 minutes before serving.

Pumpkin-spice Bread Pudding

Servings: 6
Cooking Time: 35 Minutes
Ingredients:

- Bread Pudding:
- 175 ml heavy whipping cream
- 120 g canned pumpkin
- 80 ml whole milk
- 65 g granulated sugar
- 1 large egg plus 1 yolk
- ½ teaspoon pumpkin pie spice
- ⅛ teaspoon kosher, or coarse sea salt
- 1/3 loaf of day-old baguette or crusty country bread, cubed
- 4 tablespoons unsalted butter, melted
- Sauce:
- 80 ml pure maple syrup
- 1 tablespoon unsalted butter
- 120 ml heavy whipping cream
- ½ teaspoon pure vanilla extract

Directions:

1. For the bread pudding: In a medium bowl, combine the cream, pumpkin, milk, sugar, egg and yolk, pumpkin pie spice, and salt. Whisk until well combined. 2. In a large bowl, toss the bread cubes with the melted butter. Add the pumpkin mixture and gently toss until the ingredients are well combined. 3. Transfer the mixture to a baking pan. Place the pan in the zone 1 air fryer drawer. Set the temperature to 176ºC cooking for 35 minutes, or until custard is set in the middle. 4. Meanwhile, for the sauce: In a small saucepan, combine the syrup and butter. Heat over medium heat, stirring, until the butter melts. Stir in the cream and simmer, stirring often, until the sauce has thickened, about 15 minutes. Stir in the vanilla. Remove the pudding from the air fryer. 5. Let the pudding stand for 10 minutes before serving with the warm sauce.

Healthy Semolina Pudding

Servings: 4
Cooking Time: 20 Minutes
Ingredients:

- 45g semolina
- 1 tsp vanilla
- 500ml milk
- 115g caster sugar

Directions:

1. Mix semolina and ½ cup milk in a bowl. Slowly add the remaining milk, sugar, and vanilla and mix well.
2. Pour the mixture into four greased ramekins.
3. Insert a crisper plate in the Tefal air fryer baskets.
4. Place ramekins in both baskets.
5. Select zone 1, then select "air fry" mode and set the temperature to 300 degrees F for 20 minutes. Press "match" to match zone 2 settings to zone 1. Press "start/stop" to begin.

Nutrition:

- (Per serving) Calories 209 | Fat 2.7g |Sodium 58mg | Carbs 41.5g | Fiber 0.6g | Sugar 30.6g | Protein 5.8g

Chocolate Mug Cakes

Servings: 4
Cooking Time: 20 Minutes
Ingredients:
- 1 cup flour
- 8 tablespoons sugar
- 1 teaspoon baking powder
- ½ teaspoon baking soda
- ¼ teaspoon salt
- 8 tablespoons milk
- 8 tablespoons applesauce
- 2 tablespoons vegetable oil
- 1 teaspoon vanilla extract
- 8 tablespoons chocolate chips

Directions:
1. Press "Zone 1" and "Zone 2" and then rotate the knob for each zone to select "Bake".
2. Set the temperature to 375 degrees F/ 190 degrees C for both zones and then set the time for 5 minutes to preheat.
3. In a bowl, mix together the flour, sugar, baking powder, baking soda and salt.
4. Add the milk, applesauce, oil and vanilla extract and mix until well combined.
5. Gently fold in the chocolate chips.
6. Divide the mixture into 4 heatproof mugs.
7. After preheating, arrange 2 mugs into the basket of each zone.
8. Slide each basket into Air Fryer and set the time for 17 minutes.
9. After cooking time is completed, remove the mugs from Air Fryer.
10. Place the mugs onto a wire rack to cool for about 10 minutes before serving.

Apple Hand Pies

Servings: 8
Cooking Time: 21 Minutes.
Ingredients:
- 8 tablespoons butter, softened
- 12 tablespoons brown sugar
- 2 teaspoons cinnamon, ground
- 4 medium Granny Smith apples, diced
- 2 teaspoons cornstarch
- 4 teaspoons cold water
- 1 (14-oz) package pastry, 9-inch crust pie
- Cooking spray
- 1 tablespoon grapeseed oil

- ½ cup powdered sugar
- 2 teaspoons milk

Directions:
1. Toss apples with brown sugar, butter, and cinnamon in a suitable skillet.
2. Place the skillet over medium heat and stir cook for 5 minutes.
3. Mix cornstarch with cold water in a small bowl.
4. Add cornstarch mixture into the apple and cook for 1 minute until it thickens.
5. Remove this filling from the heat and allow it to cool.
6. Unroll the pie crust and spray on a floured surface.
7. Cut the dough into 16 equal rectangles.
8. Wet the edges of the 8 rectangles with water and divide the apple filling at the center of these rectangles.
9. Place the other 8 rectangles on top and crimp the edges with a fork, then make 2-3 slashes on top.
10. Place 4 small pies in each of the crisper plate.
11. Return the crisper plate to the Tefal Dual Zone Air Fryer.
12. Choose the Air Fry mode for Zone 1 and set the temperature to 390 degrees F and the time to 17 minutes.
13. Select the "MATCH" button to copy the settings for Zone 2.
14. Initiate cooking by pressing the START/STOP button.
15. Flip the pies once cooked halfway through, and resume cooking.
16. Meanwhile, mix sugar with milk.
17. Pour this mixture over the apple pies.
18. Serve fresh.

Nutrition:
- (Per serving) Calories 284 | Fat 16g |Sodium 252mg | Carbs 31.6g | Fiber 0.9g | Sugar 6.6g | Protein 3.7g

Simple Pineapple Sticks And Crispy Pineapple Rings

Servings: 9
Cooking Time: 10 Minutes
Ingredients:
- Simple Pineapple Sticks:
- ½ fresh pineapple, cut into sticks
- 25 g desiccated coconut
- Crispy Pineapple Rings:
- 240 ml rice milk
- 85 g plain flour
- 120 ml water
- 25 g unsweetened flaked coconut
- 4 tablespoons granulated sugar
- ½ teaspoon baking soda
- ½ teaspoon baking powder
- ½ teaspoon vanilla essence
- ½ teaspoon ground cinnamon
- ¼ teaspoon ground star anise
- Pinch of kosher, or coarse sea salt
- 1 medium pineapple, peeled and sliced

Directions:
1. Simple Pineapple Sticks :
2. Preheat the air fryer to 204°C.
3. Coat the pineapple sticks in the desiccated coconut and put in the zone 1 air fryer drawer.
4. Air fry for 10 minutes.
5. Serve immediately
6. Crispy Pineapple Rings :
7. Preheat the air fryer to 204°C.
8. In a large bowl, stir together all the ingredients except the pineapple.
9. Dip each pineapple slice into the batter until evenly coated.
10. Arrange the pineapple slices in the zone 2 drawer and air fry for 6 to 8 minutes until golden brown.
11. Remove from the drawer to a plate and cool for 5 minutes before serving warm

Apple Pie Rolls

Servings: 8
Cooking Time: 12 Minutes
Ingredients:
- 3 cups tart apples, peeled, cored and chopped
- ½ cup light brown sugar
- 2½ teaspoon ground cinnamon, divided
- 1 teaspoon corn starch
- 8 egg roll wrappers
- ½ cup cream cheese, softened
- Non-stick cooking spray
- 2 tablespoons sugar

Directions:
1. In a small bowl, mix together the apples, brown sugar, 1 teaspoon of cinnamon and corn starch.
2. Arrange 1 egg roll wrapper onto a smooth surface.
3. Spread about 1 tablespoon of cream cheese over roll, leaving 1-inch of edges.
4. Place ⅓ cup of apple mixture over one corner of a wrapper, just below the center.
5. Fold the bottom corner over filling.
6. With wet fingers, moisten the remaining wrapper edges.
7. Fold side corners toward center over the filling.
8. Roll egg roll up tightly and with your fingers, press at tip to seal.
9. Repeat with the remaining wrappers, cream cheese and filling.
10. Spray the rolls with cooking spray evenly.
11. Press "Zone 1" and "Zone 2" and then rotate the knob for each zone to select "Air Fry".
12. Set the temperature to 400 degrees F/ 200 degrees C for both zones and then set the time for 5 minutes to preheat.
13. After preheating, arrange 4 rolls into the basket of each zone.
14. Slide each basket into Air Fryer and set the time for 12 minutes.
15. While cooking, flip the rolls once halfway through and spray with the cooking spray.
16. Meanwhile, in a shallow dish, mix together the sugar and remaining cinnamon.
17. After cooking time is completed, remove the rolls from Air Fryer.
18. Coat the rolls with sugar mixture and serve.

Strawberry Nutella Hand Pies

Servings: 8
Cooking Time: 15 Minutes
Ingredients:

- 1 tube pie crust dough
- 3–4 strawberries, finely chopped
- Nutella
- Sugar
- Coconut oil cooking spray

Directions:

1. Roll out the pie dough and place it on a baking sheet. Cut out hearts using a 3-inch heart-shaped cookie cutter as precisely as possible.
2. Gather the leftover dough into a ball and roll it out thinly to make a few more heart shapes. For 8 hand pies, I was able to get 16 hearts from one tube of pie crust.
3. Set aside a baking tray lined with parchment paper.
4. Spread a dollop of Nutella on one of the hearts. Add a few strawberry pieces to the mix. Add a pinch of sugar to the top.
5. Place another heart on top and use a fork to tightly crimp the edges. Gently poke holes in the top of the pie with a fork. Place on a baking sheet. Repeat for all the pies.
6. All of the pies on the tray should be sprayed with coconut oil.
7. Install a crisper plate in both drawers. Place half the pies in the zone 1 drawer and half in zone 2's, then insert the drawers into the unit.
8. Select zone 1, select BAKE, set temperature to 390°F, and set time to 10 minutes. Select MATCH to match zone 2 settings to zone 1. Press the START/STOP button to begin cooking.

Chocolate Cookies

Servings: 18
Cooking Time: 7 Minutes
Ingredients:

- 96g flour
- 57g butter, softened
- 15ml milk
- 7.5g cocoa powder
- 80g chocolate chips
- ½ tsp vanilla
- 35g sugar
- ¼ tsp baking soda
- Pinch of salt

Directions:

1. In a bowl, mix flour, cocoa powder, sugar, baking soda, vanilla, butter, milk, and salt until well combined.
2. Add chocolate chips and mix well.
3. Insert a crisper plate in Tefal air fryer baskets.
4. Make cookies from the mixture and place in both baskets.
5. Select zone 1 then select "air fry" mode and set the temperature to 360 degrees F for 7 minutes. Press "match" to match zone 2 settings to zone 1. Press "start/stop" to begin.

Nutrition:

- (Per serving) Calories 82 | Fat 4.1g |Sodium 47mg | Carbs 10.7g | Fiber 0.4g | Sugar 6.2g | Protein 1g

Peanut Butter, Honey & Banana Toast

Servings: 4
Cooking Time: 9 Minutes
Ingredients:

- 2 tablespoons unsalted butter, softened
- 4 slices white bread
- 4 tablespoons peanut butter
- 2 bananas, peeled and thinly sliced
- 4 tablespoons honey
- 1 teaspoon ground cinnamon

Directions:

1. Spread butter on one side of each slice of bread, then peanut butter on the other side. Arrange the banana slices on top of the peanut butter sides of each slice . Drizzle honey on top of the banana and sprinkle with cinnamon.
2. Cut each slice in half lengthwise so that it will better fit into the air fryer basket. Arrange the bread slices, butter sides down, in the two air fryer baskets. Set the air fryer to 190°C cooking for 5 minutes. Then set the air fryer to 205°C and cook for an additional 4 minutes, or until the bananas have started to brown. Serve hot.

Cinnamon Sugar Dessert Fries

Servings: 4
Cooking Time: 15 Minutes
Ingredients:

- 2 sweet potatoes
- 1 tablespoon butter, melted
- 1 teaspoon butter, melted
- 2 tablespoons sugar
- ½ teaspoon ground cinnamon

Directions:

1. Peel and cut the sweet potatoes into skinny fries.
2. Coat the fries with 1 tablespoon of butter.
3. Install a crisper plate into each drawer. Place half the sweet potatoes in the zone 1 drawer and half in zone 2's, then insert the drawers into the unit.
4. Select zone 1, select AIR FRY, set temperature to 390°F, and set time to 15 minutes. Select MATCH to match zone 2 settings to zone 1. Press the START/STOP button to begin cooking.
5. When the time reaches 11 minutes, press START/STOP to pause the unit. Remove the drawers and flip the fries. Re-insert the drawers into the unit and press START/STOP to resume cooking.
6. Meanwhile, mix the 1 teaspoon of butter, the sugar, and the cinnamon in a large bowl.
7. When the fries are done, add them to the bowl, and toss them to coat.
8. Serve and enjoy!

Stuffed Apples

Servings: 8
Cooking Time: 10 Minutes
Ingredients:

- 8 small firm apples, cored
- 1 cup golden raisins
- 1 cup blanched almonds
- 4 tablespoons sugar
- ¼ teaspoon ground cinnamon

Directions:

1. In a food processor, add raisins, almonds, sugar and cinnamon and pulse until chopped.
2. Carefully stuff each apple with raisin mixture.
3. Line each basket of "Zone 1" and "Zone 2" with parchment paper.
4. Press "Zone 1" and "Zone 2" and then rotate the knob for each zone to select "Air Fry".
5. Set the temperature to 355 degrees F/ 180 degrees C for both zones and then set the time for 5 minutes to preheat.

6. After preheating, arrange 4 apples into the basket of each zone.
7. Slide each basket into Air Fryer and set the time for 10 minutes.
8. After cooking time is completed, remove the apples from Air Fryer.
9. Transfer the apples onto plates and set aside to cool slightly before serving.

Baked Apples

Servings: 4
Cooking Time: 20 Minutes
Ingredients:

- 4 granny smith apples, halved and cored
- ¼ cup old-fashioned oats (not the instant kind)
- 1 tablespoon butter, melted
- 2 tablespoon brown sugar
- ½ teaspoon ground cinnamon
- Whipped cream, for topping (optional)

Directions:

1. Insert the crisper plates into the drawers. Lay the cored apple halves in a single layer into each of the drawers . Insert the drawers into the unit.
2. Select zone 1, select AIR FRY, set temperature to 350°F, and set time to 10 minutes. Select MATCH to match zone 2 settings to zone 1. Press the START/STOP button to begin cooking.
3. Meanwhile, mix the oats, melted butter, brown sugar, and cinnamon to form the topping.
4. Add the topping to the apple halves when they've cooked for 10 minutes.
5. Select zone 1, select BAKE, set temperature to 390°F, and set time to 22 minutes. Select MATCH to match zone 2 settings to zone 1. Press the START/STOP button to begin cooking.
6. Serve warm and enjoy!

Pumpkin Hand Pies Blueberry Hand Pies

Servings:4
Cooking Time: 15 Minutes
Ingredients:
- FOR THE PUMPKIN HAND PIES
- ½ cup pumpkin pie filling (from a 15-ounce can)
- ⅓ cup half-and-half
- 1 large egg
- ½ refrigerated pie crust (from a 14.1-ounce package)
- 1 large egg yolk
- 1 tablespoon whole milk
- FOR THE BLUEBERRY HAND PIES
- ¼ cup blueberries
- 2 tablespoons granulated sugar
- 1 tablespoon grated lemon zest (optional)
- ¼ teaspoon cornstarch
- 1 teaspoon fresh lemon juice
- ⅛ teaspoon kosher salt
- ½ refrigerated pie crust (from a 14.1-ounce package)
- 1 large egg yolk
- 1 tablespoon whole milk
- ½ teaspoon turbinado sugar

Directions:
1. To prep the pumpkin hand pies: In a small bowl, mix the pumpkin pie filling, half-and-half, and whole egg until well combined and smooth.
2. Cut the dough in half to form two wedges. Divide the pumpkin pie filling between the wedges. Fold the crust over to completely encase the filling. Using a fork, crimp the edges, forming a tight seal.
3. In a small bowl, whisk together the egg yolk and milk. Brush over the pastry. Carefully cut two small vents in the top of each pie.
4. To prep the blueberry hand pies: In a small bowl, combine the blueberries, granulated sugar, lemon zest (if using), cornstarch, lemon juice, and salt.
5. Cut the dough in half to form two wedges. Divide the blueberry filling between the wedges. Fold the crust over to completely encase the filling. Using a fork, crimp the edges, forming a tight seal.
6. In a small bowl, whisk together the egg yolk and milk. Brush over the pastry. Sprinkle with the turbinado sugar. Carefully cut two small vents in the top of each pie.
7. To cook the hand pies: Install a crisper plate in each of the two baskets. Place the pumpkin hand pies in the Zone 1 basket and insert the basket in the unit. Place the blueberry hand pies in the Zone 2 basket and insert the basket in the unit.
8. Select Zone 1, select AIR FRY, set the temperature to 350°F, and set the timer to 15 minutes. Select MATCH COOK to match Zone 2 settings to Zone 1.
9. Press START/PAUSE to begin cooking.
10. When cooking is complete, the pie crust should be crisp and golden brown and the filling bubbling.
11. Let the hand pies cool for at least 30 minutes before serving.
Nutrition:
- (Per serving) Calories: 588; Total fat: 33g; Saturated fat: 14g; Carbohydrates: 68g; Fiber: 0.5g; Protein: 10g; Sodium: 583mg

S'mores Dip With Cinnamon-sugar Tortillas

Servings:4
Cooking Time: 5 Minutes
Ingredients:
- FOR THE S'MORES DIP
- ½ cup chocolate-hazelnut spread
- ¼ cup milk chocolate or white chocolate chips
- ¼ cup graham cracker crumbs
- ½ cup mini marshmallows
- FOR THE CINNAMON-SUGAR TORTILLAS
- 4 (6-inch) flour tortillas
- Butter-flavored cooking spray
- 1 teaspoon granulated sugar
- ½ teaspoon ground cinnamon
- ¼ teaspoon ground cardamom (optional)

Directions:
1. To prep the s'mores dip: Spread the chocolate-hazelnut spread in the bottom of a shallow ovenproof ramekin or dish.
2. Scatter the chocolate chips and graham cracker crumbs over the top. Arrange the marshmallows in a single layer on top of the crumbs.
3. To prep the tortillas: Spray both sides of each tortilla with cooking spray. Cut each tortilla into 8 wedges and sprinkle both sides evenly with sugar, cinnamon, and cardamom (if using).
4. To cook the dip and tortillas: Install a crisper plate in each of the two baskets. Place the ramekin in the Zone 1 basket and insert the basket in the unit. Place the tortillas in the Zone 2 basket and insert the basket in the unit.
5. Select Zone 1, select BAKE, set the temperature to 330°F, and set the timer to 5 minutes.
6. Select Zone 2, select AIR FRY, set the temperature to 375°F, and set the timer to 5 minutes. Select SMART FINISH.
7. Press START/PAUSE to begin cooking.
8. When the Zone 2 timer reads 3 minutes, press START/PAUSE. Remove the basket and shake it to

redistribute the chips. Reinsert the basket and press START/PAUSE to resume cooking.

9. When cooking is complete, the dip will be bubbling and golden brown and the chips crispy.

10. If desired, toast the marshmallows more: Select Zone 1, select AIR BROIL, set the temperature to 450°F, and set the timer to 1 minute. Cook until the marshmallows are deep golden brown.

11. Let the dip cool for 2 to 3 minutes. Serve with the cinnamon-sugar tortilla chips.

Nutrition:

• (Per serving) Calories: 404; Total fat: 18g; Saturated fat: 7g; Carbohydrates: 54g; Fiber: 2.5g; Protein: 6g; Sodium: 346mg

Molten Chocolate Almond Cakes

Servings: 3
Cooking Time: 13 Minutes
Ingredients:

• Butter and flour for the ramekins
• 110 g bittersweet chocolate, chopped
• 110 gunsalted butter
• 2 eggs
• 2 egg yolks
• 50 g granulated sugar
• ½ teaspoon pure vanilla extract, or almond extract
• 1 tablespoon plain flour
• 3 tablespoons ground almonds
• 8 to 12 semisweet chocolate discs (or 4 chunks of chocolate)
• Cocoa powder or icing sugar, for dusting
• Toasted almonds, coarsely chopped

Directions:

1. Butter and flour three ramekins.

2. Melt the chocolate and butter together, either in the microwave or in a double boiler. In a separate bowl, beat the eggs, egg yolks and sugar together until light and smooth. Add the vanilla extract. Whisk the chocolate mixture into the egg mixture. Stir in the flour and ground almonds.

3. Preheat the air fryer to 165°C.

4. Transfer the batter carefully to the buttered ramekins, filling halfway. Place two or three chocolate discs in the center of the batter and then fill the ramekins to ½-inch below the top with the remaining batter. Place the ramekins into the zone 1 air fryer basket and air fry for 13 minutes. The sides of the cake should be set, but the centers should be slightly soft. Remove the ramekins from the air fryer and let the cakes sit for 5 minutes.

5. Run a butter knife around the edge of the ramekins and invert the cakes onto a plate. Lift the ramekin off the plate slowly and carefully so that the cake doesn't break. Dust with cocoa powder or icing sugar and serve with a scoop of ice cream and some coarsely chopped toasted almonds.

Homemade Mint Pie And Strawberry Pecan Pie

Servings: 8
Cooking Time: 25 Minutes
Ingredients:

• Homemade Mint Pie:
• 1 tablespoon instant coffee
• 2 tablespoons almond butter, softened
• 2 tablespoons granulated sweetener
• 1 teaspoon dried mint
• 3 eggs, beaten
• 1 teaspoon dried spearmint
• 4 teaspoons coconut flour
• Cooking spray
• Strawberry Pecan Pie:
• 190 g whole shelled pecans
• 1 tablespoon unsalted butter, softened
• 240 ml heavy whipping cream
• 12 medium fresh strawberries, hulled
• 2 tablespoons sour cream

Directions:

1. Make the Homemade Mint Pie:

2. Spray the zone 1 air fryer drawer with cooking spray.

3. Then mix all ingredients in the mixer bowl.

4. When you get a smooth mixture, transfer it in the zone 1 air fryer drawer. Flatten it gently. Cook the pie at 185°C for 25 minutes.

5. Make the Strawberry Pecan Pie:

6. Place pecans and butter into a food processor and pulse ten times until a dough forms. Press dough into the bottom of an ungreased round nonstick baking dish.

7. Place dish into the zone 2 air fryer drawer. Adjust the temperature to 160°C and set the timer for 10 minutes. Crust will be firm and golden when done. Let cool 20 minutes.

8. In a large bowl, whisk cream until fluffy and doubled in size, about 2 minutes.

9. In a separate large bowl, mash strawberries until mostly liquid. Fold strawberries and sour cream into whipped cream.

10. Spoon mixture into cooled crust, cover, and place in refrigerator for at least 30 minutes to set. Serve chilled.

RECIPES INDEX

Printed in Great Britain
by Amazon